# Cooking with Riesling

## 75 Remarkable Riesling Recipes

by

Barbara and Norm Ray

**Rayve Productions**
Hoffman Press division

**On the cover:** Riesling grapes

Cover design: Randall F. Ray
Interior illustrations: William J. Geer

Rayve Productions Inc.
Hoffman Press division
Box 726, Windsor, CA 95492

Quantity discounts and bulk purchases of this and other Hoffman Press books are available through Rayve Productions Inc. For more information and to place orders call toll-free 1-800-852-4890 or fax 707-838-2220.

Library of Congress Cataloging-in-Publication Data

Ray, Barbara, 1941 -
    Cooking with Riesling : 75 remarkable Riesling recipes / by
    Barbara and Norm Ray.
        p. cm.
    Includes index.
    ISBN 1-877810-56-8 (alk.paper)
    1. Cookery (Wine) 2. Riesling (Wine). I. Ray, Norm. II. Title

    TX726.R37728 2005
    641.6'22--dc22

                                                        2004061389

*To Virginia,*

*a continuing inspiration*

# Introduction to Riesling

Riesling, which originated in Germany, is one of the world's favorite white wines. Varying from very dry to sweet, high-quality Rieslings are praised for their delicate yet complex characterics that offer a spicy, fruity flavor, a flower-scented bouquet, and a delightfully lingering finish.

However, the the name "Riesling" is used for various wines, which can be confusing. For instance, in the United States White Riesling, also known as Johannisberg Riesling, is a pure Riesling. It is the highest quality, vinified from true Riesling grape root stock that is difficult to grow. Other Riesling wines are made from more grower-friendly hybrid Riesling grapes. And Grey Riesling isn't Riesling at all but carries the name because it has similar qualities.

As with all wines, the quality of Rieslings are determined by the source appellation, viticultural area, vintage, winemaking techniques, and numerous other subtle factors. Fine young Rieslings are fresh and fragrant, pale green, and delicate. More mature Rieslings are fuller-bodied, heavier, softer, fruitier, golden, and so rich in sugar they improve with age when properly stored.

We recommend taste-testing Riesling wines — crisp, dry White or Johannisberg Rieslings, well-balanced hybrid-Riesling vintages, rich late-harvest Rieslings and sweet Riesling ice wines. You'll discover that Rieslings are remarkably versatile wines, delicious alone, in cooking, or as an accompaniment to a wide variety of foods, from mild appetizers to spicy exotic cuisine.

# Cooking with Wine Can Be Good for Your Health

You can reduce the amount of calories, sodium, fat and cholesterol dramatically when you cook with wine. Wine adds a richness to food that easily replaces high calorie ingredients. Using dessert as an example, fruit that is poached in wine and served with a cookie or two has less than half the calories of a slice of chocolate cake.

You may use less salt, too, when you cook with wine. We enjoy the flavor of coarsely ground kosher salt or sea salt, but if you prefer little or no salt, don't use it. Salt can usually be replaced by the flavorful nuances of the ingredients in the dish when combined with wine. You can also greatly reduce the amount of fats and oil that you use very simply. In place of the usual butter, margarine or cooking oil, use a few drops of olive oil or a spritz or two of cooking oil to cook meat, poultry or fish, then use wine liberally to complete the cooking by poaching instead of frying.

When frying foods, you can easily make a sauce that will be a true gourmet's delight ... with fat and calories greatly reduced. Simply combine wine with the browned bits from the pan, and stir in a little flour to thicken the sauce.

Cholesterol levels, too, are greatly decreased and the natural goodness of your dish is enhanced when wine is used in place of cheese, cream, butter and fat.

It's nice to know that it is possible to eat well, drink well, and enjoy better nutrition, too, isn't it?

# Cooking-with-Wine Basics

**You can't cook well with bad wine.** Nothing has ever been found that equals wine in cooking, but you can't cook well with bad wine. If a Riesling tastes vinegary, sharp, raw or unpleasant, throw it out. A small amount of bad wine can ruin a dish, just as one rotten apple can spoil a barrelful.

**Cook with wine you enjoy.** The most important guide in choosing a specific Riesling for your cooking is your taste buds. It's a good idea to review published wine evaluations and talk with wine experts about various brands of Riesling, but, ultimately, you should select a good-quality wine that tastes good to you. If you don't like the taste, don't use it! Cooking will not hide or enhance the flavor; in fact, it will intensify it.

**You don't need expensive vintage wine for cooking.** It is important to cook with a moderately priced *good-quality* wine, but not necessarily an expensive *great* wine. The rich subtleties of a great wine's bouquets and flavors, which are so enjoyable when sipping, may be lost or greatly diminished when blended with herbs, spices, and other cooking ingredients and subjected to heat. So, use the good-quality Riesling for your cooking, and serve the expensive vintage to accompany it.

**Add the wine when the recipe calls for it.** *When* you add the wine to the other ingredients is crucial. Don't add it too soon, or too late. Wine performs in certain ways under certain conditions. For example, a beef stew will usually call for the wine to be added early in the recipe so it can marinate the meat, blend with other seasonings, and evaporate its alcohol during cooking.

On the other hand, a soup or dessert may require that wine be added just before it is served to provide the whole flavor of the wine, which would be dispelled if cooked.

**Add Riesling to suit your taste.** When adding Riesling to your own recipes, begin with the following portions and add more wine as desired.

<u>Quantity of Riesling Wine</u>

**Soups**
| | |
|---|---|
| Cream, Clear | 1 teaspoon per portion |
| Vegetable, Meat | 1 teaspoon per portion |

**Meats**
| | |
|---|---|
| Beef, Lamb, Veal | ¼ cup per pound |
| Ham, baked | 2 cups for basting |

**Pastas**
| | |
|---|---|
| Sauce | ¼ cup per portion |

**Poultry**
| | |
|---|---|
| Chicken, Turkey, roasted | ½ cup per pound for basting |
| Chicken, poached | ½ cup per pound for basting |
| Duck, Game Hen | ¼ cup per portion for basting |

**Seafood**
| | |
|---|---|
| Fish, broiled, baked, poached | ¼ cup per pound |
| Fish, sautéed | 4 tablespoons per pound |
| Shellfish | ¼ cup per pound |

**Fruits & Vegetables**
| | |
|---|---|
| Fresh Fruit | 1 teaspoon per portion |
| Cooked Vegetables | 1 teaspoon per portion |
| Salads | 1 teaspoon per portion |

**Most important of all, enjoy yourself!** We do, and we hope that you, too, will enjoy preparing the recipes in this book and creating new recipes using Riesling wines. Cooking with wine is a joyous adventure!

*Barbara and Norm Ray*

# Serving Wine

Serving wine correctly adds class to any occasion. Following are tips to give you added confidence when serving your guests.

**Temperature:** Riesling and other white wines require chilling. Place them in the refrigerator for two hours before serving. If you need to chill a bottle of wine quickly, place it in the freezer for 35 minutes. After opening the wine, if it's warm in the room, place the bottle half submerged in a bucket of ice to keep it well chilled.

**Wine glasses:** Riesling tastes better in a tulip-shaped stemmed wine glass with a minimum capacity of 8-10 ounces. The glass should be clear to allow guests to examine the wine's color and body, and it should curve in at the top to retain the wine's bouquet. Hold the glass by the stem to prevent heat from your hand warming the wine.

**Pouring wine:** Riesling should be poured towards the center of the glass. To prevent drips, twist the bottle slightly as you tilt it upright. Fill the glass about two-thirds full, allowing room to swirl the wine and smell its bouquet. At a dinner party, serve wine to women and older guests first, then to men, and, finally, fill your own glass.

## FRONT LABEL

① **Our Own Brand**

② **2003**

③ *Reserve*

④ *Estate Bottled*

⑤ *Our Own Vineyard*

⑥ *The American Valley*

⑦ **RIESLING**

⑧ *Net contents 750ml 13.5% alcohol*

⑨ *Vinted & bottled by Our Own Winery*
*Wineland, WV, USA*

## BACK LABEL

Vinted and Bottled by Our Own Winery, Wineland, WV, USA

⑩ Government warning: (1) According to the Surgeon General, women should not drink alcoholic beverages during pregnancy due to the risk of birth defects. (2) Consumption of alcoholic beverages impairs your ability to drive a car or operate machinery and may cause health problems. Contains sulfites.

⑪ The grapes for this wine were grown in our vineyards and vinted in our own winery by members of the same family that planted the original grape vines in 1835. We hope that you will enjoy this wine as much as we did in making it for you.

x

# The Label on the Bottle

A wine bottle label, by law, must provide an accurate description of the wine. That is mandatory. But there is usually a great deal more on the label than that. Here is a guide to reading and understanding terms you'll find on wine bottle labels.

**1. The brand name.** These days one winery may produce multiple varieties of wines under different labels. Some are secondary lines of wines ... not necessarily inferior, but possibly with less aging, or tank fermented instead of barrel fermented, etc. Other labels may represent a new wine available only in limited quantities.

**2. The date.** If there is a date on the bottle, it refers to the year the grapes were harvested and the wine made from those grapes, not simply the year in which the wine was made. In the United States, the wine label may list the vintage year if 95 percent of the wine comes from grapes crushed that year.

**3. Reserve.** This is a term used, by choice, by some vintners to indicate something special about the wine. It may be great grapes, quality barrel aging, or other unique feature.

**4. Estate bottled.** This term came from France where wineries were traditionally located where the vineyards were. In the United States, where many vineyards are miles away from the winery, "Estate Bottled" indicates that the winery either owns or controls the vineyard and is responsible for the growing of the grapes used in this bottle of wine.

**5. The vineyard name.** The vineyard name on a wine bottle label indicates that very high-quality grapes were used in the making of that wine. Vineyard designation is purely voluntary on the part of the winery.

**6. The appellation.** This is a legally protected name under which a wine may be sold, indicating that the grapes used are of a specific kind and are grown in a specific geographic area. By law, 85% of the grapes used in the production of the wine must come from that region.

**7. The name of the wine.** The wine name may be 1) a grape varietal, such as Chardonnay, Merlot, etc., 2) the name given by the winery to a specific blend of wines, such as Meritage, or 3) a simple proprietary name such as "Red Table Wine."

**8. The size of the bottle and the alcohol content.** The standard wine bottle is 750 ml. (25.4 oz.), a half bottle is 375 ml., and a split, or one-quarter bottle, is 187 ml. By law, American wines may not contain more than 14% alcohol by volume.

**9. The name and address of the bottler.**

**10. Contains sulfites.** Most wines contain sulphur dioxide, a preservative that is added to the wine. Listing all additives on the label is a legal requirement.

**11. The message.** Many wineries use back labels, too. Here you'll often find useful information about the wine, what flavors it embodies, foods it will pair well with, and other useful facts. Read the back label. It will be helpful in choosing the right wine for the right meal at the right price.

# Contents

Soups & Salads

# Simple Riesling Soup

2    **tablespoons butter**
1    **garlic clove, finely minced**
2    **tablespoons all-purpose flour**
2    **cups Riesling wine**
2    **cups vegetable broth**
4    **cups half-and-half or light cream**
2    **teaspoons kosher- or sea salt**
1    **teaspoon white pepper**
    **Chopped chives for garnish**
    **Garlic-butter croutons for garnish**

In a large saucepan over medium heat, melt butter. Sauté garlic until it is soft. Add flour and cook, stirring, for 2-3 minutes. Gradually stir in Riesling, broth, and cream. Increase heat, bring to a boil, then reduce heat and simmer, stirring continuously, until thickened. Stir in salt and pepper.

Serve hot or at room temperature. Top individual servings with chopped chives and croutons.

Serves 6

**Serve with Riesling.**

Geer

# Corn Chowder

*Use leftover baked or boiled potatoes to make this a quick-as-a-wink starter for your meal.*

| | |
|---|---|
| 3 | tablespoons butter |
| 1 | medium onion, sliced into thin rings |
| 1 | garlic clove, minced |
| 1 | cup whole kernel corn |
| 1 | cup creamed corn |
| 1 | cup diced, cooked potato |
| 1 | 10¾-ounce can cream of chicken soup |
| 2 | cups milk |
| ½ | cup Riesling wine |
| | Salt and pepper to taste |
| | Paprika for garnish |

In a large saucepan over medium heat, melt butter and sauté onion and garlic until soft. Add remaining ingredients, stir, and heat but do not boil. Adjust seasonings, adding more wine, if desired.

Lightly sprinkle individual servings with paprika.

Serves 6-8

**Serve with Riesling.**

## Wednesday Waldorf Salad

*This variation of the classic Waldorf salad is easy to prepare and a great way to use leftover meat from the weekend. Refrigerated, it keeps nicely for a couple of days.*

| | |
|---|---|
| 1 | cup chopped cooked chicken, turkey or ham |
| 1 | cup finely chopped celery |
| 1 | cup finely chopped Granny Smith or other crisp, tart green apple |
| 2 | tablespoons finely chopped red onion |
| ¼ | cup finely chopped walnuts or other favorite nuts |
| ¼ | cup dried cranberries |
| 1 | cup cooked small-sized pasta |
| ¼ | cup Riesling wine |
| 2 | teaspoons lemon juice |
| 1 | cup mayonnaise |
| ½ | cup sour cream |
| ½ | teaspoon kosher- or sea salt |
| ¼ | teaspoon pepper |
| | Fresh mint sprigs for garnish |

Combine meat, celery, apple, onion, nuts, dried cranberries, and pasta.

Blend together Riesling wine, lemon juice, mayonnaise, sour cream, salt, and pepper. Adjust seasonings to taste and stir into meat mixture. Chill salad for 45 minutes or longer.

Serve on crisp lettuce leaves on individual serving plates.

Serves 4-6

**Serve with Riesling.**

# Riesling-Mushroom Soup

1    pound porcini mushrooms
1    tablespoon butter
1    tablespoon all-purpose flour
2    cups dry Riesling wine
6    cups chicken stock
1    teaspoon kosher- or sea salt
½    teaspoon pepper
½    teaspoon dried nutmeg
6    tablespoons heavy cream
     Chopped parsley for garnish

Trim the ends of mushroom stems. Rinse mushrooms under running water, pat dry, and slice thinly.

In a 4-quart saucepan over medium heat, melt the butter and sauté mushrooms until they are golden and no longer releasing moisture. Blend in flour and stir until bubbly. Gradually stir in Riesling wine and chicken stock and bring to a boil. Add salt, pepper, and nutmeg. Lower heat and simmer, covered, for 30 minutes, stirring occasionally.

Carefully pour hot soup into a food processor or blender and purée at high speed, about 1 minute. Return the soup to the pan and bring just to the boiling point. Reduce heat, stir in cream and heat for 1 minute more. Pour into a tureen or individual bowls and serve immediately. Garnish with chopped parsley.

Serves 4

**Serve with a dry Riesling.**

# Greek Lemon Chicken Soup

6    **cups chicken broth**
2    **cups dry Riesling wine**
½    **cup lemon juice**
1    **teaspoon kosher- or sea salt**
½    **teaspoon ground pepper**
½    **cup uncooked white rice**
1    **medium carrot, shredded**
4    **egg yolks**
1    **cup chopped cooked chicken**
1    **lemon, thinly sliced, for garnish**
1    **medium carrot, grated, for garnish**

In a large saucepan over medium-high heat, combine chicken broth, Riesling wine, lemon juice, salt, and pepper. Bring to a boil. Add rice and carrot. Reduce heat, cover, and simmer 25 minutes, until rice and carrots are tender.

In a small, heatproof bowl, beat egg yolks until blended. Remove ½-cup hot soup and gradually whisk into egg yolks. Stir back into soup. Add chicken and heat through. (**Note:** Do not allow to boil again or eggs will curdle.)

To serve, ladle into individual bowls and garnish with lemon slices and grated carrot.

Serves 8

**Serve with dry Riesling.**

# Tuscan Chicken Soup

| | |
|---|---|
| 2 | tablespoons olive oil |
| 1 | clove garlic, minced |
| 2 | tomatoes, peeled and chopped (seeding optional) |
| 1 | cup chopped cooked chicken |
| 6 | cups chicken broth |
| 2 | cups dry Riesling wine |
| 1 | teaspoon dried rosemary |
| 1 | teaspoon kosher- or sea salt |
| ½ | teaspoon pepper, white pepper if you have it |
| ½ | cup tiny pasta shells |
| 2 | 16-ounce cans garbanzo beans (chick peas), rinsed and drained |
| | Paprika for garnish |

In a large saucepan over medium heat, heat olive oil, add garlic and sauté until soft. Stir in tomatoes, chicken, chicken stock, Riesling wine, rosemary, salt, and pepper. Simmer, covered, for 20 minutes.

Meanwhile, cook pasta shells according to package directions. Drain.

Using a food processor or blender, purée garbanzo beans. Ladle 1 cup chicken broth into garbanzo bean purée and process until smooth, then pour into soup and stir to blend. Add cooked pasta shells to soup. Simmer, uncovered, for 5 minutes. Sprinkle with paprika before serving.

Serves 6-8

**Serve with a dry Riesling.**

# Easy Turkey Soup

2    pounds bone-in turkey parts
1    teaspoon kosher- or sea salt
½    teaspoon pepper
1    bay leaf
1    teaspoon dried parsley
3    onions
4    stalks celery
2    cups dry Riesling wine
1½   cups diced or sliced carrot
1½   cups diced potato
1½   cups sliced zucchini

In a large saucepan over medium-high heat, combine turkey, salt, pepper, bay leaf, parsley, 2 of the onions (quartered), and 2 celery stalks. Add wine and enough water to cover ingredients. Cook, covered, just until soup boils, then reduce heat and simmer for 2 hours or until meat can be separated from the bone. Remove from heat; let cool.

When cool enough to handle meat, strain and measure broth into a separate container. Discard cooked vegetables. Pick meat from turkey bones; leave in saucepan. Add additional water and wine to broth to make 2 quarts; pour over turkey. Chop remaining onion and celery stalks. Add to broth, along with diced carrot and potato.

Simmer for 15 minutes. Add zucchini and continue simmering until vegetables are tender. Add more salt if desired.

Serves 6

**Serve with dry Riesling.**

# Cold Cucumber Soup

*In grocery stores, unwaxed English cucumbers are usually protected in clear plastic wrap. They are a bit more expensive than the standard field-grown cucumber, but this hot-house variety is seedless, burpless, and does not require peeling.*

| | |
|---|---|
| 4 | English cucumbers, unpeeled |
| 8 | green onions, sliced |
| ¼ | cup fresh dill, loosely packed |
| 3 | cups plain yogurt |
| 1 | cup Riesling wine |
| 1 | teaspoon lemon juice |
| ½ | teaspoon kosher- or sea salt |
| ¼ | teaspoon white pepper |
| | Milk as needed to thin soup |
| | Finely chopped fresh dill for garnish |

Cut unpeeled cucumbers in half lengthwise and run a spoon along the centers to remove seeds. Cut into pieces.

Using a food processor finely chop cucumber, dill, and green onions. Blend in yogurt, wine, lemon juice, salt and pepper. Thin with milk to desired consistency.
Adjust seasonings and chill.

Serve in chilled bowls. Garnish soup with dill.

Serves 6 to 8

**Serve with Riesling.**

# Watercress Salad with Riesling Dressing

4    bunches watercress
¼    cup Riesling wine
¼    cup lemon juice
2    teaspoons minced chives or scallions
½    teaspoon kosher- or sea salt
¼    teaspoon freshly ground pepper
1½  cups walnut oil
2    Golden Delicious apples, cored and diced
½    cup golden raisins
½    cup coarsely chopped walnuts

Wash and clean watercress. (Use only the freshest sprigs in your salad.) Place in a large serving bowl; chill.

Whisk together Riesling wine, lemon juice, chives, salt, and pepper. Slowly whisk in walnut oil. Adjust seasonings to taste.

To serve, toss chilled watercress with some of the dressing, using just enough to coat the leaves lightly. Gently stir in apples, raisins, and walnuts, tossing with more dressing, if desired.

Serves 8

**Serve with Riesling.**

Geer

# Four Bean Bang

| | |
|---|---|
| 1 | 15-ounce can red kidney beans |
| 1 | 15-ounce can garbanzo beans (chick peas) |
| 1 | 15-ounce can pinto beans |
| 1 | 15-ounce can black beans |
| ¼ | cup chopped celery |
| 1 | scallion, finely chopped |
| 3 | cloves garlic, minced |
| ¼ | cup finely chopped white onion |
| 4 | teaspoons lemon juice |
| 3 | teaspoons Feta cheese |
| 1 | tablespoon oregano flakes |
| 1 | teaspoon dried oregano |
| ½ | teaspoon kosher- or sea salt |
| ½ | teaspoon pepper |
| ¾ | cup red wine vinegar |
| ¼ | cup olive oil |
| ½ | cup Riesling wine |

In a large colander, rinse and drain beans.

In a large bowl, combine remaining ingredients. Stir in beans. Cover and refrigerate for several hours or overnight. The flavor improves with longer marinating.

Serve in individual small bowls, on lettuce leaves, or tossed into a green salad.

Serves 8-10

**Serve with dry Riesling.**

# Curried Chicken and Apple Soup

*If you are adventurous, try this unusual and versatile soup.*
*It is delicious hot or cold.*

2   tablespoons butter
1   medium onion, finely chopped
1   small apple, peeled, cored, and sliced
2   teaspoons curry powder
1½  cups chicken broth
1½  cups Riesling wine
1   cup chopped cooked chicken
1   8-ounce can sliced water chestnuts, drained and
    coarsely chopped
2   cups heavy cream or half and half
4   egg yolks

In a large saucepan over medium heat, melt butter. Add onion and apple. Cook until onion is translucent, about 3 minutes. Stir in curry powder. Add chicken broth, Riesling wine, and chicken. Bring to a boil and reduce heat. Simmer, covered, for 10 minutes. Reduce heat to lowest setting. Stir in water chestnuts.

In a small, heatproof bowl, whisk cream into egg yolks. Gradually beat in 1½ cups hot soup. Stir egg mixture into soup in saucepan. (**Note:** Do not allow soup to boil again or eggs will curdle.)

Serves 6

**Enjoy with Riesling.**

Geer

# Broccoli Bisque

3    **tablespoons butter**
2    **cloves garlic, minced**
1    **cup finely chopped scallions**
1    **cup sliced mushrooms**
3    **tablespoons flour**
1½  **cups chicken broth**
1½  **cups dry Riesling wine**
1    **cup fresh broccoli florets**
1    **cup half-and-half**
1    **cup shredded Jarlsberg cheese**

In a large saucepan over medium heat, melt butter and sauté garlic, scallions, and mushrooms until tender. Add flour and cook, stirring continuously, until mixture begins to boil. Remove from heat and gradually stir in chicken broth and Riesling wine. Return to medium heat and cook, stirring continuously, until liquid is smooth and thickened.

Reduce heat to low. Add broccoli and cook until tender. Blend in cream and cheese. Simmer until soup is heated through and cheese is melted.

Serves 4

**Serve with Riesling.**

13

# Classic French Onion Soup

| | |
|---|---|
| ¼ | cup butter |
| 6 | medium onions, thinly sliced |
| 4 | cups chicken broth |
| 1 | cup dry Riesling wine |
| 1 | teaspoon kosher- or sea salt |
| ½ | teaspoon pepper |
| 6 | slices French bread, toasted and buttered |
| ½ | cup grated Parmesan cheese |

Move oven rack to upper level. Preheat oven to 450° F.

In a large saucepan over medium heat, melt butter and sauté onions until translucent. Add chicken broth and cook, covered, until onions are very tender. Stir in Riesling wine, salt, and pepper and bring to a boil.

Pour soup into 6 individual ovenproof ramekins. Place pieces of buttered French bread toast on top and sprinkle with Parmesan cheese. Bake on upper rack of oven until cheese browns lightly, about 10 minutes.

If desired, to enhance the soup's flavor, add 2 teaspoons cool dry Riesling wine to each bowl of soup just before serving.

Serves 6

**Serve with dry Riesling**

14

# Riesling Marinated Mushrooms

| | |
|---|---|
| 3 | tablespoons olive oil |
| 1 | small onion, minced |
| 3 | cloves garlic, minced |
| 1 | pound mushrooms, cleaned, stems trimmed |
| 1 | bay leaf |
| 2 | whole cloves |
| 4 | peppercorns |
| ½ | cup dry Riesling wine |
| 2 | teaspoons lemon juice |
| 1 | teaspoon kosher- or sea salt |
| ¼ | teaspoon freshly ground pepper |

In a large saucepan over medium heat, heat oil and sauté onion and garlic until soft. Stir in mushrooms, bay leaf, cloves, and peppercorns. Add Riesling, lemon juice, salt, and pepper. Reduce heat to medium-low and cook, covered, until mushrooms are crisp-tender, about 10 to 15 minutes. Remove pan from heat and let cool.

When cooked mushrooms are cool, remove them with a slotted spoon. Discard bay leaf, peppercorns, and cloves.

Over medium-high heat, uncovered, simmer remaining marinade until it is reduced by half. Pour over mushrooms. Adjust seasonings. Serve on individual plates with toasted sourdough baguette slices, or combine with salad.

Serves 6

**Serve with Riesling.**

# Hollywood Turkey Salad

*Belgium endive or spinach may be used in place of some of the leaf lettuce.*

| | |
|---|---|
| 1 | pound smoked turkey breast, cut in ½-inch pieces |
| ½ | head red leaf lettuce |
| ½ | head green leaf lettuce |
| ½ | bunch watercress |
| 1 | cup each red and green seedless grapes |
| ¾ | cup slivered almonds, chopped pecans, or other favorite nut meat |

**DRESSING**

| | |
|---|---|
| 1 | ounce blue cheese |
| 2 | tablespoons Riesling wine |
| 1 | teaspoon Dijon mustard |
| ⅓ | cup olive oil |
| ¼ | cup heavy cream (whipping cream) |

In a large bowl, combine turkey, lettuce, watercress, grapes, and nuts. Toss gently. Refrigerate.

For salad dressing, use a blender to purée blue cheese, Riesling wine, and Dijon mustard. With motor running, slowly add olive oil. Transfer to a small bowl and whisk in heavy cream, and salt and pepper to taste. Sprinkle lightly on turkey salad.

Serves 6

**Serve with Riesling.**

16

Pastas &
Grains

# Baked Rice with Cheese and Mushrooms

1     cup uncooked rice
6     tablespoons butter, divided
4     tablespoons flour
2     cups milk
1     cup grated American cheese, divided
1     cup fresh mushrooms
1     cup sliced pimiento-stuffed olives
1     small green pepper, finely chopped
4     hard-cooked eggs, sliced
      Salt and pepper to taste
¼     cup Riesling wine

Preheat oven to 375° F. Steam rice according to package directions.

<u>**White sauce:**</u> In a medium pan over medium heat, melt 4 tablespoons of the butter, gradually stir in flour and, stirring continuously, heat until bubbly. Gradually add milk and continue to stir until sauce thickens slightly. Add ½ cup of the cheese and stir until melted. Remove from heat.

In a small pan, sauté mushrooms in remaining butter. Combine cooked rice and white sauce. Add mushrooms and remaining ingredients in order given. Pour into greased individual casseroles or one large casserole, and sprinkle top with remaining cheese.

Bake for 25 to 30 minutes.

Serves 6

**Serve with Riesling.**

# Super Spinach Rice

| | |
|---|---|
| 2 | cups uncooked rice |
| 1 | 10-ounce package frozen chopped spinach |
| 1 | cube (¼ pound) butter |
| 1 | clove garlic, minced |
| ½ | teaspoon dried sage |
| ½ | cup Riesling wine |
| 1 | teaspoon kosher- or sea salt |
| ½ | cup grated Parmesan cheese |

Steam rice according to package directions.

Cook spinach according to package directions. Drain.

In a medium skillet over medium heat, melt butter and sauté garlic and sage, being careful not to let the butter become brown. Stir in Riesling wine and salt. Remove from heat; keep warm.

Transfer steamed rice to a large bowl. Pour wine sauce over rice; mix well. Reheat drained spinach for 45 seconds in microwave oven; blend into rice. Sprinkle with cheese and serve.

This dish is excellent with roast turkey or game hen.

Serves 4

**Serve with Riesling.**

19

# Rice Genovese

2    cups uncooked rice
¼    cup olive oil
½    cup onion, minced
4    slices bacon, diced
4    sweet Italian sausages, casings removed, minced
1    6-ounce jar marinated artichoke hearts, drained and coarsely chopped
1    cup frozen peas
½    pound mushrooms, sliced
1    teaspoon fresh parsley, chopped
½    teaspoon rosemary
½    teaspoon oregano
½    teaspoon kosher- or sea salt
¼    teaspoon black pepper
2    cups beef or chicken broth
1    cup Riesling wine
½    cup grated Parmesan cheese, divided
3    tablespoons butter, melted
1    tablespoon bread crumbs
3    tablespoons melted butter

Preheat oven to 375° F. Steam rice according to package directions.

In a 4-quart saucepan over medium heat, heat olive oil and sauté onion until translucent; set aside. In same pan, sauté bacon and sausages until meat is brown. Add sautéed onion, artichokes, peas, mushrooms, parsley, rosemary, oregano, salt, and pepper. Cover and simmer for 5 minutes. Stir in broth and Riesling. Cover and simmer for 30 minutes.

Add rice to cooked ingredients. Mix well and add three tablespoons Parmesan cheese. Place in buttered casserole and bake for 15 minutes. Remove from oven, sprinkle with remaining cheese, bread crumbs, and melted butter. Return to oven for 15 minutes more.

Serves 6

**Serve with Riesling.**

# Quick Broccoli Pasta

| | |
|---|---|
| 1 | pound spaghetti or other favorite pasta |
| ½ | cup olive oil |
| 1½ | pounds fresh broccoli |
| 2 | cloves garlic |
| 1½ | cups Riesling wine |
| 1 | teaspoon kosher- or sea salt |
| ½ | teaspoon black pepper |
| | Parmesan cheese for garnish |

Cook pasta according to package directions; keep warm.

In a medium pan over medium heat, heat olive oil and sauté garlic until translucent. Add broccoli; simmer, uncovered, for 4 to 5 minutes, stirring occasionally. Add wine, salt, and pepper; cover and cook until broccoli is crisp tender.

Place cooked pasta on individual serving plates and top with broccoli. Sprinkle with Parmesan cheese.

Serves 4

**Serve with Riesling.**

# Polenta with Chicken

| | |
|---|---|
| 1 | package refrigerated polenta (or cook your own polenta with corn meal, if preferred) |
| 3 | slices bacon, diced |
| 4 | tablespoons butter |
| 1 | pound mushrooms, sliced |
| 1 | small red bell pepper, chopped |
| 2 | cups cooked, chopped chicken breast |
| ½ | cup Riesling wine |
| ¼ | teaspoon sage |
| 1 | teaspoon kosher- or sea salt |
| | Chopped fresh parsley for garnish |

Slice polenta and cook according to package directions, or prepare polenta from scratch. Keep warm.

In a large skillet over medium-high heat, sauté bacon until crisp. Reduce heat to medium. Stir in butter. When butter melts, add mushrooms and red bell pepper and sauté for 1 to 2 minutes. Add chicken, Riesling wine, sage, and salt. Reduce heat and cook for 2 or 3 minutes more. Adjust seasonings to taste.

To serve, place polenta in a ring around the outside edge of a large platter. Place chicken and mushrooms in the center of the platter and pour the pan juices over the polenta. Sprinkle with chopped parsley.

Serves 4-6

**Serve with Riesling.**

# Linguine with Roasted Vegetables

1  package linguine
3  cups apple juice
1  cup Riesling wine
1  clove garlic, peeled
3  tablespoons butter
1¼  pounds turnips
1¼  pounds parsnips
1¼  pounds carrots
1¼  pounds red-skinned sweet potatoes (yams)
1¼  pounds rutabagas
1  teaspoon kosher- or sea salt
½  teaspoon black pepper

Preheat oven to 425° F.

In a large saucepan over medium-high heat, bring apple juice and Riesling wine to a boil. Add whole garlic clove. Simmer, uncovered, for about 30 minutes, until liquid is reduced to ¾ cup. Remove from heat, discard garlic clove, and whisk in butter.

Peel and cut vegetables into ½-inch pieces. Divide between 2 large roasting pans. Pour wine-apple juice mixture over vegetables. Sprinkle with salt and pepper. Toss to coat. Roast until vegetables are tender and golden, stirring occasionally, about 40 minutes.

Meanwhile, cook linguine according to package directions. Drain and transfer to a serving platter. Top with vegetables.

Serves 8

**Serve with Riesling.**

23

# Riesling-Clam Lasagna

*Prepare this dish the day before your event, refrigerate, and pop in the oven an hour before guests arrive.*

| | |
|---|---|
| 8 | ounces uncooked lasagna noodles |
| 2 | 6½-ounce cans minced clams |
| 4 | tablespoons butter |
| ¼ | cup all-purpose flour |
| 1 | 8-ounce bottle clam juice |
| 2 | cloves garlic, minced |
| 2 | teaspoons Italian herb seasoning |
| ¼ | cup lightly packed, finely chopped, fresh parsley |
| ¼ | cup Riesling wine |
| 1 | pint ricotta cheese |
| 1 | 10-ounce package frozen chopped spinach, thawed, liquid squeezed out |
| ½ | pound jack cheese, thinly sliced |
| ½ | cup Parmesan cheese |

Drain clams, reserving liquid; set aside.

In a 3-quart pan over medium heat, melt butter. Add flour and cook, stirring continuously, until bubbly. Gradually stir in reserved clam liquid and clam juice. Continue cooking and stirring until mixture boils and thickens (about 5 minutes). Remove from heat and stir in clams, garlic, herb seasoning, parsley, and Riesling wine.

Prepare lasagna noodles according to package directions. Line a greased 9 x 13-inch baking dish with a third of the noodles. Spoon ricotta cheese evenly over noodles and top with a third of the clam sauce. Add a second layer of noodles.

Arrange spinach over noodles. Cover with half of the jack cheese slices, then spread with half the remaining clam sauce. Top with remaining noodles, cheese slices, and clam sauce. (If desired, cover and refrigerate at this point.)

Before baking, sprinkle lasagna with Parmesan cheese. Bake, uncovered, in a 350° F oven for 30 minutes (45 minutes if refrigerated) or until bubbly and heated through. Let stand for 10 minutes. Cut into serving-sized pieces.

Serves 6-8

**Serve with Riesling.**

# Easy Cheddar Chicken on Noodles

1      **10½-ounce can cream of mushroom soup**
1      **10½-ounce can cream of celery soup**
1½    **cup grated sharp Cheddar cheese, divided**
¾     **cup dry Riesling wine**
6      **chicken breasts (about 3 pounds), boned and skinned**
½     **cup sliced green onions for garnish**
1      **package noodles, cooked**

Preheat oven to 350° F.

In a large shallow baking pan, combine soups, 1 cup of cheese, and wine. Add chicken. Cover pan with foil; bake for 45 minutes to 1 hour or until chicken is done.

To serve, pour chicken and sauce over cooked noodles. Top with remaining ½-cup shredded cheese and green onions.

Serves 6-8

**Serve with Riesling.**

25

# Mixed Seafood Lasagna

| | |
|---|---|
| 1 | package lasagna noodles |
| 2 | cloves garlic, minced |
| 6 | tablespoons butter |
| ¼ | cup all-purpose flour |
| 1 | tablespoon Italian seasoning |
| 1 | teaspoon kosher- or sea salt |
| ¼ | teaspoon pepper |
| 2 | cups milk |
| 2 | cups Riesling wine |
| 1 | pound cooked shrimp |
| 1 | pound cooked crab or imitation crab |
| 2 | cups ricotta cheese |
| 2 | tablespoons lemon juice |
| 1½ | cups Parmesan cheese, divided |

Preheat oven to 375° F.

In a medium-sized saucepan over medium heat, melt butter and sauté garlic until it is soft. Stir in flour, Italian seasoning, salt, and pepper; stir until smooth and bubbly. Gradually stir in milk and Riesling until smooth. Heat to a boil stirring continuously; boil for 1 minute. Remove from heat and stir in shrimp and crab. Set aside.

In a medium-sized bowl, combine ricotta cheese, ¾-cup parmesan cheese, and lemon juice. Set aside.

Prepare lasagna noodles according to package directions. When noodles are cool enough to handle, spread 1 cup of the seafood mixture in the bottom of a 9 x 13-inch pan.

Place a layer of cooked lasagna noodles over sauce. Top with ricotta mixture. Continue layering until ingredients are used. (Top layer should be seafood sauce.)

Cover pan with foil; bake for 30 minutes. Uncover and bake 10 more minutes. Sprinkle with remaining Parmesan cheese. Let stand 10 minutes before serving.

Serves 10-12

**Serve with Riesling.**

# Fettucine Romanoff

1   **8-ounce package fettucine**
3   **cups large-curd cottage cheese**
2   **cloves garlic, minced**
½   **cup Riesling wine**
2   **teaspoons Worcestershire sauce**
2   **cups sour cream**
6   **green onions, finely chopped**
½   **teaspoon bottled hot sauce**
1   **cup grated Parmesan cheese**

Preheat oven to 350° F.

Cook fettucine according to package direction; drain. Mix remaining ingredients into pasta and pour into a buttered 2-quart casserole. Bake for 25 minutes.

Serves 6

**Serve with Riesling.**

## Spinach and Tomato Fettuccine

| | |
|---|---|
| 1 | 9-ounce package uncooked refrigerated fettuccine |
| 2 | tablespoons butter |
| 1 | clove garlic, minced |
| ½ | cup pine nuts |
| ½ | teaspoon kosher- or sea salt |
| ¼ | teaspoon black pepper |
| ½ | cup Riesling wine |
| 1 | 10-ounce bag fresh spinach, stems removed |
| 6 | Roma tomatoes, cut into eighths |

Cook fettuccine according to package directions. Drain and keep warm.

In a 4-quart saucepan over medium heat, melt butter and sauté garlic and pine nuts until garlic is soft and nuts are lightly browned. Stir in salt and pepper.

Stir in Riesling wine and spinach and continue cooking until spinach is limp (2 to 3 minutes). Add tomatoes. Continue cooking until heated through.

Spoon spinach mixture over cooked fettuccine; sprinkle with Parmesan cheese.

Serves 4

**Serve with Riesling.**

# Spaghetti with Herbed Chicken

| | |
|---|---|
| 1 | chicken (3 pounds), washed, patted dry, and cut into serving pieces |
| | Salt and pepper |
| 3 | tablespoons olive oil |
| 1 | large onion, thickly sliced |
| 3 | cloves garlic, minced |
| ½ | pound mushrooms, sliced |
| 1 | tablespoon chopped fresh parsley |
| ½ | teaspoon dried thyme |
| ½ | teaspoon dried rosemary |
| 2 | large tomatoes, chopped |
| ½ | cup dry Riesling wine |
| 1 | 8-ounce package uncooked spaghetti |
| | Grated Parmesan cheese for garnish |

Season chicken with salt and pepper. In a large, deep skillet over medium-high heat, sauté meat in olive oil until lightly browned, about 8 minutes. Remove from pan; keep warm.

Remove all but 3 tablespoons fat from skillet. Sauté onions, garlic, and mushrooms until tender. Reduce heat to medium. Return chicken to skillet. Sprinkle with parsley, thyme, and rosemary. Add tomatoes and Riesling. Simmer, partly covered, for 45 to 50 minutes, until chicken is tender.

Meanwhile, prepare spaghetti according to package directions. To serve, place spaghetti on a large platter, top with chicken and sauce. Sprinkle with Parmesan cheese.

Serves 4 to 6

**Serve with Riesling.**

# Artichoke-Mushroom Pasta

1    6-ounce jar marinated artichoke hearts, drained, reserving liquid, coarsely chopped.
½    pound fresh mushrooms, sliced
1    tablespoon grated onion
2    cloves garlic, minced
1    15-ounce can tomato sauce
½    cup Riesling wine
1    tablespoon lemon juice
1    2¼-ounce can sliced black olives, drained
2    teaspoons dried basil
2    teaspoons dried oregano
1    teaspoon kosher- or sea salt
¼    teaspoon freshly ground black pepper
1    pound spaghetti or other favorite pasta
      Freshly grated Parmesan cheese

In a large sauté pan over medium-high heat, bring reserved liquid from artichokes to a boil. Add mushrooms, onion, and garlic and sauté over high heat for 5 minutes. Add artichokes and remaining ingredients (except pasta). Simmer, uncovered, for 20 minutes. Adjust seasonings, adding more Riesling if desired.

Prepare pasta according to package directions. Pour sauce over pasta, and sprinkle liberally with Parmesan cheese. Serve with green salad and crusty sourdough bread.

Serves 6

**Serve with Riesling.**

# Italian Rice Croquettes

2    **cups uncooked rice**
3    **tablespoons tomato sauce**
¼    **cup Riesling wine**
4    **tablespoons butter**
½    **cup grated Parmesan cheese**
2    **eggs, beaten**
1    **cup diced mozzarella cheese**
1½    **cups fine bread crumbs**
2    **cups olive oil**

Cook rice in salted boiling water until tender but still firm, about 15 minutes. Drain and let cool.

Mix cooled rice with tomato sauce, Riesling wine, butter, Parmesan cheese, and eggs. Shape into oblong croquettes by spreading 1 tablespoon of rice in palm of hand; place 1 piece of mozzarella cheese in center of rice; top with 1 tablespoon rice. Roll in bread crumbs. Repeat until all rice is used.

In a large pan over medium-high heat, heat olive oil and fry a few croquettes at a time, turning to brown all sides.

Serve hot as part of antipasto or with meat or fowl.

Serves 6-8

**Serve with Riesling.**

# Chile Macaroni and Cheese with Riesling

| | |
|---|---|
| 2 | cups uncooked macaroni |
| 2 | tablespoons soft butter |
| 1½ | cups cubed sharp cheddar cheese |
| ½ | teaspoon kosher- or sea salt |
| ½ | teaspoon dry mustard |
| 2 | eggs, beaten |
| 1½ | cups half and half |
| ½ | cup Riesling wine |
| 3 | tablespoons chopped canned green chiles |
| 1 | 2-ounce jar chopped pimientos |
| ½ | cup dry bread crumbs mixed with melted butter |

Preheat oven to 350° F.

Combine all ingredients except bread crumbs; mix well. Place in a buttered 1½-quart baking dish. Sprinkle with buttered bread crumbs. Cover baking dish with aluminum foil and bake for 40 to 50 minutes. Let stand 5 to 10 minutes before serving, to thicken liquid in casserole.

Serves 6

**Serve with Riesling.**

# Meats

# Veal Stew with Mushrooms and Broccoli

4   tablespoons butter
1   medium onion, diced
3   slices bacon, diced
2   pounds veal rump, cut into 1½-inch cubes
½   cup Riesling wine
2   tablespoons tomato paste
1   cup beef or chicken broth
1   teaspoon kosher- or sea salt
½   teaspoon black pepper
8   ounces small fresh mushrooms
1½  pounds fresh broccoli florets

In a 3-4 quart pan over medium-high heat, melt butter and sauté onion and bacon until soft. Add veal and brown on all sides. Stir in Riesling wine. Simmer, uncovered, until wine has evaporated.

Blend tomato paste, broth, salt, and pepper. Pour over meat. Reduce heat, cover pan, and simmer stew for 1 hour, adding a little broth or water if meat gets dry.

Add mushrooms and broccoli and simmer for 15 minutes more.

Serves 6

**Serve with Riesling.**

34

# French Country Steak

2    rib steaks (about 1¼-pounds each)
2    teaspoons kosher- or sea salt
1    teaspoon ground pepper
1    tablespoon vegetable oil
2    ounces butter, one piece
4    ounces (1 cube) butter, cut in half; chop one of the halves in small pieces
4    shallots, finely chopped
1    pound small mushrooms, cleaned, stems trimmed
½    cup dry Riesling wine
1    tablespoon chopped fresh parsley

Pat the steaks dry and season with salt and pepper.

In a large skillet over medium-high heat, heat the oil. Add a single 2 ounce-piece of butter and, as soon as it melts, add the steaks and cook to desired doneness. (A couple of minutes per side is usually adequate.) Remove steaks from pan and keep warm.

In same skillet over medium heat, add shallots and Riesling, and mushrooms. Sauté just until mushrooms are tender; remove them from pan; keep warm. Increase heat to high and cook liquid in skillet, stirring continuously, scraping up browned bits, until liquid is reduced to 2 tablespoons.

Remove pan from heat and whisk in remaining butter, one piece at a time, until light and foamy. Add chopped parsley and pour sauce over steaks. Serve with mushrooms.

Serves 4

**Serve with dry Riesling.**

# Veal Rolls with Goat Cheese

**12 to 18 slices of veal, pounded very thin**
**12 to 18 slices of pancetta**
**4    ounces soft goat cheese**
**     Dried dill**
**     Salt and pepper**
**3    tablespoons butter**
**3    tablespoons olive oil**
**1½  cups dry Riesling wine**

On each slice of veal, place a slice of pancetta, and top with a half-teaspoon of goat cheese. Sprinkle lightly with salt, pepper, and dill. Roll jelly-roll fashion and secure with a toothpick. Continue this process until all slices of meat have been used. If preparing for later use, cover and refrigerate at this point.

To cook, use a large skillet over medium-high heat. Heat butter and oil and sauté veal rolls for 1 to 2 minutes on each side. Remove from pan and keep warm.

In same skillet over high heat, add wine and bring to a boil. Boil for several minutes, stirring continuously, scraping up browned bits, until liquid is slightly reduced. Return the veal rolls to the pan, rolling them briefly in the reduced wine sauce.

To serve, arrange veal on a platter and cover with wine sauce.

Serves 6

**Serve with Riesling.**

# Spanish Pork Chops

4    **loin pork chops**
½    **cup uncooked rice**
4    **medium onions, thinly sliced**
2½  **cups canned, ready-cut tomatoes**
1    **teaspoon kosher- or sea salt**
½    **teaspoon pepper**
1    **cup dry Riesling wine**
      **Tomato slices or cherry tomatoes for garnish**
      **Fresh parsley for garnish**

Preheat oven to 350° F.

Arrange pork chops in a large buttered casserole or glass baking dish. Place a heaping tablespoon of uncooked rice on each chop. Cover with alternate layers of sliced onions and tomatoes. Season with salt and pepper.

Pour the Riesling wine over all. Cover and bake for 1 to 1½ hours, basting occasionally with juices in the pan. Add more wine if it bakes dry. Remove cover for the last 15 minutes so meat will brown.

Transfer pork chops to a serving platter. Surround with tomatoes and garnish with fresh parsley.

Serves 6

**Serve with Riesling.**

# Fricassee of Rabbit with Mushrooms

| | |
|---|---|
| 1 | rabbit, cut into 8 pieces |
| 1 | tablespoon fresh thyme leaves |
| | Salt and pepper to taste |
| ¾ | olive oil |
| 2 | large cloves garlic, minced |
| 2 | bay leaves |
| ½ | cup Riesling wine |
| 1 | cup chicken broth |
| 1 | cup creme fraiche (pg. 76) or heavy whipping cream |
| 1 | pound mushrooms, sliced |
| 2 | tablespoons butter |
| 2 | tablespoons chopped fresh parsley for garnish |

Sprinkle rabbit with thyme, salt, and pepper. Pour oil into a large saucepan over medium-high heat and sauté rabbit until golden brown. Remove meat from pan; pour off oil.

Return rabbit meat to pan. Add garlic, bay leaves, Riesling wine, chicken broth, and creme fraiche. Simmer, covered, for approximately 1 hour or until rabbit is very tender.

Meanwhile, in a small skillet over medium heat, melt butter and sauté mushrooms. Add mushrooms to rabbit during the last 10 minutes of cooking.

To serve, arrange fricassee of rabbit on a platter and garnish with chopped parsley.

Serves 4

**Serve with Riesling.**

# Herbed Veal in Creamy Riesling Sauce

2    pounds lean veal
1¼   teaspoons dried Italian seasoning
½    teaspoon dried marjoram leaves
¼    teaspoon garlic salt
¼    teaspoon nutmeg
1    teaspoon all-purpose flour
½    teaspoon kosher- or sea salt
3    tablespoons butter
2    teaspoons cornstarch
½    cup water
½    cup half and half
½    cup dry Riesling wine

Cut veal into thin strips (¼ x ½ x 1¼ inches). Combine Italian seasoning, marjoram, garlic salt, nutmeg, flour, and salt.

In a large skillet over high heat, melt butter. Add meat, sprinkle with seasoning mixture, and sauté, stirring frequently, until meat is browned on all sides.

Reduce heat to low. Stir cornstarch into 1 tablespoon of the water. Add remaining water to cornstarch mixture. Pour over meat, stirring continuously. Stir in cream and wine. Cover and cook 10 minutes or until mixture thickens slightly. Do not boil.

Serve over rice or noodles.

Serves 6

**Serve with dry Riesling.**

# Shredded Beef with Vegetables

1     4-pound piece rump roast or cross rib of beef
3     large carrots, peeled
8     medium onions: 2 halved; 6 thinly sliced
2     cloves garlic, minced
1     bay leaf
10    peppercorns
4     tablespoons butter, divided
     Salt and pepper
1     bottle Dry Riesling wine, as needed
     Dry bread crumbs

In a large saucepan over medium-high heat, place meat, carrots, 2 halved-onions, bay leaf, and peppercorns. Cover with water. Bring to a boil. Reduce heat and simmer, covered, for 3 to 4 hours. Skim off foam from time to time. Cool meat in cooking liquid. Discard bay leaf.

When meat is cool, remove from pan, reserving broth. Shred meat by picking it apart with two forks. (DO NOT CUT!)

In a large, deep skillet over medium-high heat, melt 2-tablespoons butter and sauté sliced onions and garlic until golden brown. Mix well with shredded beef; season with salt and pepper, and place in a 2- to 3-inch deep baking dish.

Measure cooking broth; add an equal amount of wine. Pour into pan in which onions and garlic were sautéed. Bring to a boil; simmer, uncovered, until liquid is slightly reduced, 5 to 10 minutes. Pour over meat; sprinkle generously with bread crumbs; dot with butter. Bake in 350° F oven for 45 minutes.

Serves 8

**Good with Dry Riesling**

# Quick and Easy Fruited Ham

1    center slice of ham, ¾-inch thick
½    tablespoon butter
1    medium-sized orange, peeled and sliced
1    cup seedless green grapes, halved if large
½    cup Late Harvest Riesling wine
    Juice of 1 lemon
    Chopped fresh parsley for garnish

Trim excess fat from ham.

In a large skillet over medium-high heat, melt butter and brown ham. Add orange slices and grapes; sauté for 1 minute. Place fruit on top of ham.

Stir together Riesling wine and lemon juice; pour over ham and fruit. Reduce heat and simmer, uncovered, 10 minutes. If wine cooks away, add a little more wine or water to maintain moisture in pan.

Transfer ham to serving platter; arrange orange slices and grapes around ham; keep warm.

Deglaze skillet, scraping up browned bits; simmer until sauce is slightly reduced and thickened. Add a little more salt and wine, if desired. Pour hot wine sauce over ham and fruit. Garnish with chopped parsley.

Serves 4

**Serve with Late Harvest Riesling.**

# Minty Greek Meat Patties

*These flavorful patties, which are crisp on the outside and moist on the inside, are delicious hot or cold.*

2    **eggs**
1½  **cups soft bread crumbs**
1    **large onion, grated**
1    **clove garlic, minced**
¼   **cup Riesling wine**
     **Juice of 1 lemon**
2    **tablespoons chopped fresh parsley**
2    **teaspoons dried mint or 1 tablespoon fresh chopped mint**
1    **teaspoon kosher- or sea salt**
½   **teaspoon pepper**
1    **pound ground lamb or veal**
     **All-purpose flour for dredging patties**
     **Olive oil for frying patties**

In a small, deep mixing bowl, beat eggs lightly. Stir in bread crumbs, onion, garlic, Riesling wine, and lemon juice, parsley, mint, salt, and pepper. Let sit 10 minutes. Add meat and blend thoroughly. Cover and refrigerate 1 hour.

With moistened hands, shape meat mixture into 2-inch balls. Roll in flour and flatten to make thick patties. Fry in hot olive oil, a few at a time, until golden brown, 3 to 4 minutes per side. Drain on paper towels. Transfer to a serving dish and keep warm until all patties are cooked.

Makes about 24 patties

**Serve with Riesling.**

# Curried Lamb Shanks

½  cup olive oil
8  medium-sized lamb shanks
½  cup flour
1  tablespoon curry powder
1¼ cups water
1  cup dry Riesling wine
2  teaspoons kosher- or sea salt
¼  teaspoon black pepper
1  clove garlic, minced
1  white or yellow onion, sliced

In a large, heavy saucepan, heat olive oil to high and sauté lamb shanks until they are golden brown on all sides. Remove shanks from pan.

In the same saucepan, blend flour and curry powder into drippings. Add water and Riesling wine. Cook, stirring continuously, until mixture is thickened and smooth. Add more wine, if necessary, to make a smooth paste. Stir in salt, pepper, and garlic.

Return lamb shanks to pan; add onion slices. Simmer, covered, for 1½ hours, or until meat is tender.

This dish is delicious with rice, sautéed fresh vegetables, a lightly dressed green salad, and garlic bread.

Serves 8

**Serve with Dry Riesling.**

# Tripe Parisienne

4½   pounds honeycomb tripe, cut in 2-inch squares
1     bottle dry Riesling wine
1     14-ounce can chicken broth
      Salt and pepper
1     bay leaf
¼     teaspoon dried thyme
1     yellow onion, chopped
4     scallions, chopped
1     pound veal shank, cut in 2-inch cubes
12    peppercorns
½     pound fresh mushrooms, halved
4     tablespoons Brandy

Place tripe, covered with lightly salted water, in a large, ovenproof Dutch oven or pan over high heat. Bring to a boil and simmer, covered, for 30 minutes. Drain thoroughly.

Return tripe to pan; cover with boiling water, Riesling wine, and chicken broth. Season with salt and pepper. Add bay leaf, thyme, onion, scallions, and parsley. Bring to a boil. Simmer, covered, for ½ hour, skimming off foam.

Add veal. Cover and bake at 250° F for 4 to 5 hours. Add more hot water and Riesling during cooking to keep meat covered with liquid.

During last 15 minutes, add peppercorns, mushrooms, and Brandy. Carefully remove bones from veal. Adjust seasonings; add more wine, if desired. Serve in a tureen or individual bowls.

Serves 6-8

**Serve with Grey Riesling.**

# Riesling and Herbs Pork Roast

| | |
|---|---|
| 4 | tablespoons all-purpose flour, divided |
| 2 | teaspoons kosher- or sea salt, divided |
| 1 | teaspoon black pepper |
| ½ | teaspoon dried thyme |
| 1 | bone-in pork loin roast (4 to 5 pounds) |
| 2 | medium onions, coarsely chopped |
| 2 | large carrots, coarsely chopped |
| 2 | bay leaves |
| 2 | cups water |
| 1½ | cup Riesling wine |
| ⅓ | cup firmly packed brown sugar |

Preheat oven to 325° F.

In a small bowl, combine 2 tablespoons flour with 1 teaspoon of salt, pepper, and thyme; rub over entire surface of roast.

Place meat, fat side up, in a roasting pan. Arrange vegetables and bay leaves around meat. Add water to pan. Bake roast, uncovered, for 1½ hours, basting frequently with pan juices.

Remove roast from oven, sprinkle with ½-cup Riesling and brown sugar. Bake 30 minutes more, or until meat thermometer reaches 160°. Place roast on a serving platter; keep warm.

Strain pan drippings, reserving broth; discard vegetables and bay leaves. Add Riesling wine to the broth to measure 1⅔ cups. Return to pan. Combine remaining 2 tablespoons flour with a little cold water until smooth; stir into pan juices; add salt. Bring to a boil; cook and stir for 2 minutes. Serve with roast.

Serves 10-12

**Serve with Riesling.**

45

# Ham Loaf with Riesling Raisin Sauce

2    **tablespoons butter**
2    **eggs, beaten**
1    **small onion, finely chopped**
1    **clove garlic, minced**
2    **cups ground cooked ham**
½    **cup bread crumbs**
2    **tablespoons catsup**
2    **tablespoons Worcestershire sauce**
¼    **teaspoon prepared mustard**
     **Salt and pepper to taste**

**SAUCE**
2    **tablespoons butter**
2    **tablespoons flour**
     **Pinch of salt**
½    **cup Late Harvest Riesling wine**
½    **cup apple cider**
¼    **cup golden raisins**

Preheat oven to 350° F.

In a large skillet over medium-high heat, melt butter. Sauté onion and garlic until soft. Place ham in a large bowl; stir in cooked onion, garlic, and remaining ingredients. Shape into a loaf and place in a well-greased loaf pan. Bake 40 minutes or until done. Transfer meat to serving platter; keep warm.

To make sauce, melt 2 tablespoons butter in a small saucepan. Add flour and salt; brown slightly. Gradually add wine and cider, stirring continuously, until sauce is smooth and thickened. Stir in raisins. Pour over ham loaf.

Serves 4-6

**Serve with Late Harvest Riesling.**

Poultry

# Chicken Rolls with Goat Cheese and Sun-Dried Tomatoes

6    ounces goat cheese
6    chicken breasts, skinned and boned, pounded to
     ¼-inch thickness
½    cup finely chopped sun-dried tomato (oil-based),
     divided
2    tablespoons chopped fresh basil
2    tablespoons butter
1    tablespoon olive oil
½    cup chicken broth
½    cup Riesling wine
     Finely chopped fresh parsley for garnish

Spread 1-ounce goat cheese over each chicken breast. Top with 1 tablespoon sun-dried tomatoes, and sprinkle with basil. Roll breasts jelly-roll style; secure with wooden toothpicks.

In a large skillet over medium heat, heat butter and olive oil. Add chicken and sauté until lightly browned outside and moist inside, 10-12 minutes. Remove from pan and keep warm.

Pour all but 1 tablespoon fat from pan. Add chicken broth, wine, and remaining sun-dried tomatoes. Over medium heat, simmer, uncovered, until liquid is reduced by half.

To serve, remove toothpicks from meat; cut crosswise on the diagonal into ½-inch slices. Arrange on a platter and spoon wine sauce over all.

Serves 6

**Serve with Riesling.**

# Chicken with Mustard Sauce

| | |
|---|---|
| 1 | cup Riesling wine |
| 2 | tablespoons butter |
| 1 | teaspoon kosher- or sea salt |
| ½ | teaspoon pepper |
| 2 | chicken breasts, skinned, boned, cut in half |
| ½ | pound fresh mushrooms, sliced |
| 2 | scallions, finely chopped |
| 2 | cloves garlic, minced |
| ½ | cup half-and-half |
| 1 | teaspoon dry mustard |
| 1 | tablespoon capers |
| ½ | teaspoon dry dill |

In a large skillet over medium-high heat, combine Riesling wine, butter, salt, and pepper. When liquid simmers, add chicken breasts and cook, covered, turning chicken once, just until breasts are no longer pink in the center, about 12 minutes. Remove chicken from skillet; keep warm.

In the same skillet over medium-high heat, add mushrooms, scallions, and garlic. Cook until mushrooms are tender and wine is reduced by half, about 5 to 10 minutes.

In a small bowl, whisk together half and half and mustard until blended. Stir into wine sauce and simmer until slightly thickened, 3 to 5 minutes. Stir in capers and dill. Adjust salt and pepper to taste.

To serve, arrange chicken breasts on a platter and top with mustard-wine sauce. Garnish with capers and dill.

Serves 4

**Serve with Riesling.**

49

# Bombay Curry

1    **pound turkey tenderloins or slices, cut into ½-inch cubes**
1    **cup cubed crisp red apple**
1    **teaspoon curry powder**
3    **teaspoons butter**
½    **cup mango chutney**
¾    **cup Riesling wine**
      **Cooked rice for 4 servings**

In a small bowl, combine turkey, apple, and curry powder; let stand for 10 minutes.

In a medium skillet over medium-high heat, stir-fry turkey mixture in butter for 2 to 3 minutes or until turkey interior is no longer pink. Remove from heat and keep warm.

In same skillet, stir in chutney and Riesling wine and simmer, stirring and scraping up browned bits from pan, until wine sauce is slightly reduced.

To serve, pour sauce over rice.

Serves 4

**Serve with Riesling.**

# Divine Cheddar Divan

*This recipe is quickly cooked in a microwave. If you prefer, use broccoli in place of the asparagus.*

| | |
|---|---|
| 2 | tablespoons butter |
| 2 | tablespoons all-purpose flour |
| ½ | cup milk |
| ½ | cup Riesling wine |
| 2 | teaspoons Dijon mustard |
| ¼ | teaspoon cayenne pepper or to taste |
| 8 | slices cooked turkey |
| 2 | cups asparagus spears, partially cooked |
| ½ | cup shredded sharp cheddar cheese |

In a 4-cup microwave-safe container, melt butter in microwave set on high, about 40 seconds. Stir in flour. Combine milk and wine and gradually stir into flour mixture. Microwave on high for 3 to 4 minutes, stirring once every minute until thick. Stir in mustard and cayenne. Set aside.

In a shallow 2½-quart, microwave-safe dish, layer turkey slices. Arrange asparagus on top with tips to center. Pour sauce over all; cover with waxed paper. Microwave on medium for 7 to 8 minutes; sprinkle cheese over top. Microwave on medium for 2 to 3 minutes more. Allow to stand, covered, for 5 minutes before serving.

Serves 4

**Serve with Riesling.**

51

# Turkey "Scallopini"

*Scallopini is a traditional Italian veal dish, but turkey can be used in the recipe with excellent results.*

| | |
|---|---|
| 1 | turkey quarter breast (about 2 pounds) or turkey breast slices, boned and skinned |
| ¼ | cup all-purpose flour |
| 1 | teaspoon kosher- or sea salt |
| ¼ | teaspoon paprika |
| ¼ | teaspoon white pepper |
| 2 | tablespoons butter, divided |
| 2 | tablespoons olive oil, divided |
| 6 | ounces (1½ cups) small mushrooms, halved |
| 1 | clove garlic, minced |
| ¾ | cup dry Riesling wine |
| 1 | tablespoon finely chopped parsley |
| 1½ | teaspoons lemon juice |
| ½ | teaspoon dried Italian seasoning |

Place turkey breast in freezer for about 1 hour or until surface of meat is thoroughly chilled and slightly firm. Cut meat in ¼-inch slices. In a medium-sized shallow bowl, combine flour, salt, paprika, and pepper. Dredge meat slices in seasoned flour mixture, shaking off excess.

In a large skillet over medium-high heat, heat half the butter and oil. Sauté turkey, a few pieces at a time, until lightly browned on all sides. Use additional butter and oil as needed. Remove turkey from skillet and keep warm.

To the same skillet, sauté mushrooms and garlic for 1 to 2 minutes. Return browned turkey to skillet.

In a small bowl, combine wine, parsley, lemon juice, and Italian seasoning. Pour over turkey and mushrooms and simmer rapidly for 5 to 10 minutes or until liquid is reduced and turkey is tender.

Serves 6

**Serve with Riesling.**

# Garlic Slow-Cooker Turkey

1¼   **pounds skinless, boneless turkey thighs**
      **Salt and pepper to taste**
1     **tablespoon olive oil**
1     **head garlic, cloves separated and peeled**
½     **cup dry Riesling wine**
½     **cup chicken broth**

Season turkey lightly with salt and generously with pepper. In a large skillet over medium-high heat, heat oil. Add thighs and brown turkey on all sides, about 10 minutes.

Place turkey in slow cooker and add remaining ingredients. Cook on medium setting for 3½ hours (or on high for 2½ hours). Remove garlic cloves. (If desired, crush garlic and return to cooker.) Serve garlic-turkey broth over meat.

Serves 5

**Serve with Riesling.**

Geer

53

# French Turkey Fillets

1   **pound skinless, boneless turkey breast fillets**
    **Salt and pepper to taste**
1   **tablespoon olive oil**
2   **tablespoons butter**
3   **tablespoons minced green onion**
1   **cup dry Riesling wine**

Season turkey fillets with salt and pepper. In a large skillet over medium-high heat, heat oil. Add fillets and cook, turning, until lightly browned, about 2 minutes on each side or until cooked through. Transfer fillets to a platter and keep warm.

In the same skillet over medium heat, melt 1 tablespoon of the butter. Sauté green onion until soft, about 1 minute. Stir in Riesling wine. Increase heat to medium-high; boil wine, uncovered, for 1 to 2 minutes or until it is reduced to a thick, syrupy sauce. Remove skillet from heat and swirl in remaining butter.

To serve, pour wine sauce over turkey fillets.

Serves 6 to 8

**Serve with Riesling.**

# Poached Turkey Tenderloins

*Cook this dish ahead and serve it when time is tight. It keeps well in the refrigerator for two days.*

| | |
|---|---|
| 2 | turkey breast tenderloins (about 1½ pounds) |
| ½ | cup chopped celery with leaves |
| ¼ | cup sliced green onion |
| 1 | teaspoon dried, crushed tarragon |
| ½ | teaspoon kosher- or sea salt |
| ¼ | teaspoon white pepper |
| ¾ | cup dry Riesling wine |

In a large skillet over medium heat, arrange turkey breast tenderloins in a single layer. Add celery, onion, tarragon, salt, pepper, and Riesling wine. Add water to just cover turkey.

Cover skillet and simmer over low heat for 40 minutes or until the interior of the tenderloins is no longer pink. Transfer tenderloins to a platter; keep warm.

In the same skillet over medium-high heat, boil liquid until it is reduced to about 1 cup. Adjust seasonings to taste, and add more Riesling wine, if desired.

Serve wine sauce over tenderloins, or store, covered, in refrigerator.

Serves 4

**Serve with Riesling.**

# Almond Crusted Turkey Steaks

1    **turkey half breast (2 pounds), skin removed**
½    **cup raw almonds, grated**
¼    **cup grated Parmesan cheese**
¼    **cup dried basil**
¼    **cup paprika**
1    **teaspoon kosher- or sea salt**
3    **tablespoons butter, divided**
3    **tablespoons olive oil, divided**
½    **cup dry Riesling wine**
2    **teaspoons lemon juice**

Cut turkey breast into ½-inch steaks parallel to top of breast. Place steaks between sheets of waxed paper and pound to about ¼-inch thickness.

Mix grated almonds with Parmesan cheese, basil, paprika, and salt on sheet of waxed paper. Dip turkey steaks, one at a time, into mixture, coating both sides.

In a large skillet over medium heat, heat 1 tablespoon each butter and oil; sauté turkey steaks, a few at a time, until lightly browned on both sides. Use additional butter and oil as needed. Transfer turkey to a platter; keep warm.

In the same skillet over high heat, stir in wine and lemon juice; boil rapidly, stirring up browned bits, until slightly thickened. Spoon over steaks.

Serves 4 to 6

**Serve with Riesling.**

# Rock Cornish Hens in Sour Cream

2    Rock Cornish game hens
3    tablespoons butter
¾    cup sliced onions
1    teaspoon kosher- or sea salt
1    teaspoon paprika
½    teaspoon pepper
1    cup sliced mushrooms
½    cup Riesling wine
1½  cups sour cream
      Parsley for garnish

Coat hens with flour.

In a large saucepan over medium-high heat, melt butter and sauté game hens until golden brown on all sides. Add onions and sauté until tender.

In a small bowl, combine salt, paprika, and pepper; sprinkle over hens. Place mushrooms around hens. Reduce heat, cover saucepan, and simmer for 30 to 45 minutes, until hens are cooked. Transfer hens to platter; keep warm.

In the same saucepan over low heat, gradually add wine and sour cream to remaining ingredients, stirring continuously. Pour over game hens. Garnish with parsley.

Serves 2

**Serve with Riesling.**

# Two Cheese Chicken with Mushrooms

½  cup flour
½  teaspoon kosher- or sea salt
½  teaspoon garlic salt
½  teaspoon black pepper
2   eggs
¼   cup grated Parmesan cheese
4   chicken breast halves, boned and skinned
¼   cup (½ cube) butter
½   cup Riesling wine
1   cup sliced mushrooms
½   cup shredded Mozzarella cheese
¼   cup fresh chopped parsley

In a shallow dish or plastic bag, combine flour, salts, and pepper. In a separate shallow dish, beat eggs. In a third shallow dish, pour Parmesan cheese.

Dredge chicken with seasoned flour, then dip into egg, then into Parmesan cheese. If a thicker crust is desired, repeat process.

In a large skillet over medium heat, melt butter and sauté mushrooms until crisp-tender. Set aside and keep warm.

In same skillet, sauté chicken until golden brown. Add Riesling and cook, uncovered, until chicken is no longer pink in the middle, about 10 minutes. Place mushrooms on top of chicken, sprinkle Mozzarella cheese over top, cover, and cook until cheese is melted. Remove to serving platter, garnish with parsley, and serve.

Serves 4

**Serve with Riesling.**

# Peruvian Chicken

2    tablespoons butter
1    chicken (about 3 pounds), cut into serving pieces
1    small onion, chopped
1    bay leaf
½    teaspoon cumin
½    teaspoon ground cloves
1    cup chicken broth
1    teaspoon kosher- or sea salt
½    teaspoon ground black pepper
1¼  cups Riesling wine
½    cup golden raisins
½    cup sliced, blanched almonds
½    cup half-and-half
2    egg yolks

In a large, deep skillet over medium-high heat, melt butter and sauté chicken until lightly browned, about 4 minutes on each side. Add onions, bay leaf, cumin, cloves, and broth. Reduce heat and simmer, covered, for 15 minutes.

Stir in half the Riesling, raisins, and almonds. Increase heat to medium-low and cook, partly covered, for another 20 to 25 minutes, until chicken is tender. Reduce heat.

In a small, heatproof bowl, whisk together cream, egg yolks, and remaining wine. Stir ½-cup soup into cream sauce; stir back into soup on stove. Stir soup until slightly thickened. (Do not boil again.) Discard bay leaf before serving.

Serves 4

**Serve with Riesling.**

# Dilled Chicken

| | |
|---|---|
| 2 | large chicken breasts, skinned, boned, halved |
| 4 | tablespoons vegetable oil, divided |
| 1 | cucumber, peeled and thinly sliced |
| 1 | cup sliced green onions |
| ½ | cup minced fresh dill, divided |
| ½ | teaspoon kosher- or sea salt |
| ¼ | teaspoon pepper |
| ½ | pound mushrooms, end trimmed and halved |
| ½ | cup Riesling wine |
| 1 | pint sour cream |

Cut chicken breasts part way through and flatten.

In a large skillet over medium heat, heat 1 tablespoon oil. Add cucumber, scallions, and 1 tablespoon dill. Sauté until cucumber is translucent; remove from pan; sprinkle with salt.

In the same skillet, add 1 tablespoon oil, heat, and sauté mushrooms, sprinkling them with 1 tablespoon dill. Transfer mushrooms to a bowl.

In the same skillet over medium-high heat, add remaining oil. Add chicken and sauté until lightly browned, about 6 minutes. Add remaining dill, pepper, and Riesling. Reduce heat and simmer, partly covered, turning occasionally, until interior of chicken is no longer pink. Transfer chicken to a platter; keep warm.

To pan drippings, add sour cream, cucumber mixture, and mushrooms. Stir until heated through. Pour over chicken.

Serves 4

**Serve with Riesling.**

# Seafood

# Quick-as-a-Snap Snapper

2   tablespoons olive oil
1   cup thinly sliced fresh mushrooms
1   small onion, cut into thin rings
2   cloves garlic, minced
1   green bell pepper, cut into strips
3   large tomatoes, cut into wedges
1½  teaspoons dried thyme
1   teaspoon kosher- or sea salt
1   teaspoon parsley
1   pound red snapper fillets
¼   cup Riesling wine
    **Fresh chopped parsley for garnish**

Pour oil into a large skillet over medium heat. In skillet, layer mushrooms, onion, garlic, green pepper, and tomato wedges. Sprinkle with thyme, salt, and parsley.

Place fish fillets on top of vegetables and sprinkle with wine. Add additional seasonings if desired. Bring to a boil, cover, and simmer 10 to 15 minutes, or until fish flakes easily with a fork.

To serve, garnish with fresh chopped parsley.

Serves 4

**Serve with Riesling.**

# Salmon Baked in Riesling

2    **pounds salmon (six fillets or slices) or other favorite fish such as halibut, sea bass or sole**
      **Salt and pepper**
1    **large onion, sliced**
1    **cup Riesling wine**
3    **tablespoons butter**
2    **large tomatoes, sliced**
½    **large green pepper, sliced**
2    **teaspoons Worcestershire sauce**
¼    **cup fresh dill, chopped**
      **Lemon slices and fresh dill for garnish**

Sprinkle fish with salt and pepper; cover with sliced onion; pour Riesling over all and let stand for 30 minutes.

Melt butter in a large, shallow baking pan. Remove fish and onion from marinade and place in melted butter in pan. Reserve wine marinade. Cover fish with tomatoes and green pepper. Sprinkle with salt and chopped dill.

Preheat oven to 375° F oven. Bake fish until it is tender and flakes easily (about 35 minutes), basting frequently with a mixture of the reserved wine marinade and Worcestershire sauce.

To serve, garnish with lemon slices and fresh dill.

Serves 6

**Serve with Riesling.**

# Italian Fish Stew

3  pounds fresh fish, chopped into serving pieces
   (grouper or other favorite)
4  green bell peppers, chopped
4  cloves garlic, minced
2  pounds new potatoes, sliced
1  cup Riesling wine
6  large tomatoes, chopped
¼  cup olive oil
1  bunch fresh parsley, chopped
1  tablespoon dried oregano
   Parmesan cheese for garnish

In a large pot over medium-high heat, combine all ingredients. Cover and cook for 20 to 30 minutes. Reduce heat to simmer and cook for 30 minutes more.

Sprinkle liberally with Parmesan cheese when serving.

Serves 6-8

**Serve with Riesling.**

# Riesling Crab Cakes

| | |
|---|---|
| 1 | pound fresh lump crabmeat |
| 2 | tablespoons minced onion |
| 1 | clove garlic, minced |
| 1 | tablespoon minced red bell pepper |
| 1 | tablespoon minced green bell pepper |
| 2 | egg whites |
| ¾ | cup mayonnaise |
| 1 | teaspoon lemon juice |
| ¼ | cup Riesling wine |
| 1 | teaspoon dried seafood seasoning |
| 1 | teaspoon kosher- or sea salt |
| ½ | teaspoon pepper |
| | Dried bread crumbs as needed |
| | Olive oil for frying crab cakes |

In a medium-sized bowl, gently stir together the crabmeat, scallions, garlic, and bell peppers.

In a separate bowl, combine egg whites, mayonnaise, lemon juice, Riesling wine, seafood seasoning, salt and pepper. Stir until smooth.

Combine egg-white mixture with crabmeat mixture. Gradually stir in dried bread crumbs until mixture is firm enough to form into 4 cakes.

Pour additional bread crumbs in a shallow bowl or pan and roll cakes in bread crumbs. In a large skillet over medium-high heat, fry crab cakes until golden, turning once.

Makes 4 crab cakes

**Serve with Riesling.**

66

# Baked Crab-and-Shrimp Combo

8    tablespoons butter
8    tablespoons flour
6    cups milk
2    teaspoons olive oil
2    cups sliced mushrooms
1    cup diced green bell pepper
1    teaspoon paprika
1½  cups Riesling wine
     Dash of salt and black pepper
½    cup diced pimientos
1½  pound crab meat
1½  pound shrimp meat
4    teaspoons grated Parmesan cheese

Preheat oven to 375° F.

**WHITE SAUCE:** In a 4-quart saucepan over medium heat, melt butter, blend in flour and stir until bubbly. (Do not allow to brown.) Gradually add milk and cook, stirring continuously, until thickened. Remove from heat.

In a large saucepan over medium heat, heat olive oil. Add mushrooms and green bell pepper; sauté until tender. Stir in paprika and Riesling wine. Simmer, uncovered, until liquid is reduced by half. Add salt and pepper, then white sauce and pimientos; blend well. Return to simmer.

Add crab and shrimp to vegetable-wine sauce; simmer for 10 minutes. Pour into a casserole, sprinkle with Parmesan cheese, and brown in oven for 15 to 20 minutes.

Serves 4

**Serve with Riesling.**

# Pepper Jack Sole

6    tablespoons butter
2    tablespoons all-purpose flour
1½  cups milk, heated
6    sole fillets
2    cups dry Riesling wine
½    pound fresh mushrooms, finely chopped
6    tablespoons heavy cream
     Salt and pepper
½    cup dry Riesling wine
1    cup shredded pepper jack cheese
     Chopped fresh parsley for garnish

Preheat oven to 350° F.

In a medium saucepan over medium heat, melt butter, stir in flour, and gradually add heated milk. Cook, stirring continuously, until thickened. Remove from heat; cool, stirring occasionally to prevent a skin from forming.

Meanwhile, place fish in a baking dish and cover with wine. Bake for 30 minutes.

Combine mushrooms with ½ of the white sauce; pour into serving dish and keep warm. Carefully remove fillets and place them on top of mushroom sauce. To remaining white sauce, add the cream, remaining 3 tablespoons butter, salt, and pepper. Heat, but do not boil. Pour sauce over fish. Top with grated pepper jack cheese and return to the oven until cheese is melted. Sprinkle with chopped parsley.

Serves 6

**Serve with Dry Riesling.**

# Quenelles Lyonnais

*This dish is a bit more time consuming than most in this cookbook, but the end result is well worth the effort.*

1    pound pike fillets, skin and bones removed
4    eggs
1¼  cups heavy cream or half and half
1    teaspoon kosher- or sea salt
½    teaspoon black pepper
¼    cayenne pepper
4    ounces (1 cube) butter, cut into small pieces

**BEURRE BLANC SAUCE**
4    shallots, finely chopped
6    tablespoons dry Riesling wine
3    tablespoons white wine vinegar
7    ounces butter, cut into ¾-inch cubes
     Salt and pepper to taste

In a food processor, purée fish. With the machine running, add the eggs, cream, salt, black pepper, and cayenne pepper. Add the butter, piece by piece, blending until smooth. Refrigerate for 12 hours.

When fish purée is chilled, turn out on a lightly floured work surface. Shape large spoonfuls of the mixture into 6 smooth oblong shapes (quenelles); set aside.

In a 6-quart saucepan over medium-high heat, bring 3 quarts water to a simmer. Drop in the quenelles, a few at a time, and simmer for 15 minutes. Drain on paper towels, then transfer to a warmed platter; keep warm.

***Beurre Blanc* Sauce:** In a small saucepan over medium heat, combine shallots, Riesling, vinegar, and salt and pepper. Simmer, uncovered, until liquid is reduced to 2 teaspoons. Reduce heat to lowest setting. Vigorously whisk butter, cube by cube, into the reduced liquid. When all the butter has been incorporated and the sauce is light and foamy, set it aside and keep it warm.

Pour beurre blanc sauce over quenelles and serve.

Serves 6

**Serve with Riesling.**

# Quick Salmon Snack

| | |
|---|---|
| 1 | can salmon, well drained |
| 1 | tablespoon Riesling wine |
| 1 | tablespoon olive oil |
| 1 | tablespoon soy sauce |
| 2 | teaspoons wine vinegar |
| 1 | teaspoon lemon juice |
| ¼ | cup finely chopped green onion |
| 1 | 4-ounce jar chopped pimiento |
| 2 | teaspoons bottled capers (optional) |
| | Salt and pepper to taste |

Combine all ingredients and chill for several hours. Serve with crackers, toasted sourdough baguette slices, buttered dill-rye, or pumpernickel bread.

Serves 6-8

**Serve with Riesling.**

# Sautéed Tuna with Riesling Dill Sauce

8    tablespoons butter, divided
2    tablespoons chopped shallots
1    cup dry Riesling wine
1    tablespoon fresh dill
1    cup clam broth
¼    cup heavy cream (whipping cream)
     Salt and pepper
2    pounds tuna, sliced into 6 fillets (Ask your butcher
     to slice the tuna for you.)
     Lemon slices for garnish
     Fresh parsley for garnish

In a medium-sized saucepan over medium heat, melt 1 tablespoon of the butter and sauté shallots until tender. Add Riesling wine and dill. Simmer until liquid is reduced to 1 tablespoon. Add clam broth and reduce again to 2 tablespoons. Add cream and bring to a boil. Whisk in 5 tablespoons of the butter. Salt and pepper to taste. Remove from heat; keep warm.

In a large skillet over medium-high heat, sauté tuna in the remaining 2 tablespoons butter, about 3 minutes per side or until fillets flake easily with a fork.

To serve, divide tuna fillets among six plates. Ladle sauce over fillets. Garnish with lemon slices and fresh parsley.

Serves 6

**Serve with dry Riesling.**

# Poached Scallops with Tomato Concassée

| | |
|---|---|
| 6 | Roma tomatoes |
| 1 | tablespoon balsamic vinegar |
| 1 | teaspoon kosher- or sea salt |
| ½ | teaspoon pepper |
| 2 | cloves garlic, minced |
| 1 | cup clam juice |
| ½ | cup dry Riesling wine |
| 2 | tablespoons lemon juice |
| 1 | tablespoon peppercorns |
| 1 | pound scallops |

Fill a medium saucepan with water; bring to a boil. Meanwhile, fill a large bowl with ice and water. Blanch tomatoes by immersing them in the boiling water for 1 minute and then immediately immersing them in ice water. When cool enough to handle, remove tomato skins with fingers or a small knife. Beginning at stem end, cut tomatoes in half vertically; remove seeds. Finely dice tomatoes and combine with vinegar, salt, pepper, and garlic. Set aside.

In a large skillet over medium-high heat, simmer clam juice with Riesling wine, lemon juice, and peppercorns. Add scallops and cook, covered, for 5 minutes.

Heat the tomato concassée gently before serving. Remove scallops from poaching broth. Spoon concassée mixture onto individual plates and top with poached scallops. Garnish with chopped parsley.

Serves 4

**Serve with dry Riesling.**

# Rock Shrimp with Pasta

| | |
|---|---|
| 1 | pound rock shrimp, deveined |
| 2 | tablespoons olive oil |
| 2 | shallots, diced |
| 4 | cloves garlic, minced |
| 4 | Roma tomatoes, chopped |
| 2 | roasted red bell peppers, seeded and chopped |
| 1 | cup dry Riesling wine |
| 10 | capers |
| | Pinch of saffron |
| 4 | cups radiatore or other favorite pasta, cooked according to package directions |
| | Salt and pepper to taste |
| 4 | teaspoons butter |
| | Juice of half a lemon |
| ½ | cup chopped fresh basil |
| | Parmesan cheese, grated |

In a large skillet over medium heat, sauté shrimp in olive oil. Add shallots, garlic, tomatoes, and red pepper; sauté for 30 seconds more. Add Riesling wine, capers, and saffron. Simmer, uncovered, until liquid is reduced by half.

Stir in the pasta; salt and pepper to taste. Add butter and lemon juice to finish. Toss.

To serve, top with fresh basil and Parmesan cheese.

Serves 4

**Serve with dry Riesling.**

# Charcoal Grilled Shrimp on Skewers

| | |
|---|---|
| 2 | pounds shrimp, peeled and deveined |
| ½ | pound fresh mushrooms, stemmed |
| ½ | cup dry Riesling wine |
| 2 | teaspoons Dijon mustard |
| 2 | tablespoons olive oil |
| 2 | tablespoons lemon juice |
| 2 | scallions, finely chopped |
| 2 | cloves garlic, minced |
| | Dash salt and pepper |
| | Dash hot pepper sauce |
| | Melted butter for grilling |

Place shrimp and mushrooms in a shallow glass dish.

In a small bowl, stir together Riesling wine, mustard, oil, lemon juice, scallions, garlic, salt, pepper, and hot pepper sauce. Adjust seasonings to taste. Pour marinade over shrimp and mushrooms. Cover and refrigerate for several hours, spooning marinade over shrimp and mushrooms periodically.

When ready to cook, thread shrimp and mushrooms on skewers. Grill over hot charcoal until done, 8 to 10 minutes, turning and brushing often with marinade and additional melted butter.

Serves 6-8

**Serve with dry Riesling.**

# Harvest Day Trout

| | |
|---|---|
| 4 | trout, plate sized, scaled, cleaned, washed, and patted dry |
| 1½ | cups macadamia nuts, finely chopped |
| 1 | cup pitted prunes, finely chopped |
| ¼ | cup Riesling wine |
| 1½ | cups bread crumbs |
| 1 | teaspoon kosher- or sea salt |
| ½ | teaspoon black pepper |
| 1 | teaspoon chopped fresh parsley |
| 1 | teaspoon chopped fresh dill |
| 1 | teaspoon olive oil |
| ½ | teaspoon lemon juice |
| | Fresh parsley or dill for garnish |

Scale, clean, wash, and pat trout dry; set aside.

In a large bowl, mix together nuts, prunes, Riesling wine, and bread crumbs. Stir in salt, pepper, parsley and dill.

Gently press nut-fruit filling into cavity of trout, securing with toothpicks or satay skewer.

In a large skillet over medium-high heat, heat olive oil and fry trout for 3-4 minutes on each side.

Before serving, sprinkle with lemon juice and garnish with sprigs of fresh parsley or dill.

Serves 4

**Serve with Riesling.**

**Desserts**

# Nutty Raisin Cake with Creme Fraiche

| | |
|---|---|
| 1 | 15-ounce package golden raisins |
| 2½ | cups Late Harvest Riesling wine |
| 2 | tablespoons cooking oil |
| 1½ | cups sugar |
| | Pinch of salt |
| 4 | cups all-purpose flour |
| 1 | teaspoon baking soda |
| 2 | teaspoons cinnamon |
| 1 | teaspoon nutmeg |
| 1 | cup chopped walnuts |

Preheat oven to 325° F. In a large saucepan over medium-high heat, bring first 5 ingredients to a boil. Simmer, covered, 10 to 20 minutes; cool. Add sifted dry ingredients and mix thoroughly. Add nuts and mix again. Pour batter in 2 greased 5- x 9-inch loaf pans. Bake 45 minutes to 1 hour. Top cake slices with Creme Fraiche (recipe below).

Serves 12-16

**Serve with Late Harvest Riesling.**

**CREME FRAICHE (Requires 48 hours to mature)**

| | |
|---|---|
| 1 | cup heavy cream or whipping cream |
| 1 | cup dairy sour cream |

**NOTE: Prepare creme fraiche at least 2 days ahead.**
Whisk heavy cream and sour cream together until thoroughly blended. Pour into a jar, cover, and let stand in a warm place until thickened, about 12 hours. Stir well, cover, and refrigerate for 36 hours before using.

# Riesling Lemon Cream

*This exceptionally light dessert is the perfect finish to a heavy meal . . . or anytime.*

| | |
|---|---|
| 5 | eggs, separated |
| 1 | cup plus 2 tablespoons granulated sugar |
| 2 | teaspoons lemon juice |
| | Grated peel of 1 lemon |
| 1 | envelope plain gelatin |
| ¼ | cup cold water |
| ¾ | cup Late Harvest Johannisberg Riesling |
| | Mint leaves for garnish |
| | Chopped macadamia nuts for garnish |

In a large bowl, combine egg yolks, sugar, lemon juice, and grated lemon peel; beat 10 minutes on high speed.

In a small bowl, soften gelatin in cold water. In a small pan over medium heat, bring Riesling just to the boiling point; turn off heat. Pour gelatin into hot wine and stir until gelatin is dissolved. In a thin stream, slowly add gelatin-wine liquid to egg mixture.

In a separate small bowl, beat egg whites on high speed until stiff; gently fold into gelatin mixture. Chill well.

To serve, mound lemon cream in parfait or sherbet glasses. Garnish with mint leaves and nuts.

Serves 10-12

**Serve with Late Harvest Johannisberg Riesling.**

# Easy Pumpkin-Pear Trifle

1    loaf pumpkin bread (bake your own or buy a loaf at the bakery), cut into 1-inch cubes (8 cups)

2    packages vanilla pudding mix (not instant)

4    cups milk for pudding

1¼    cups Riesling wine

½    cup sugar

1½    teaspoons finely shredded lemon peel

½    teaspoon ground nutmeg

¼    teaspoon cinnamon

4    large ripe pears, peeled, cored, and cut into ½-inch slices

Whipped cream and lemon peel curls for garnish

Cook pudding according to package directions. Chill.

In a large skillet over low heat, stir together Riesling, sugar, lemon peel, nutmeg, and cinnamon. Cook and stir until sugar is dissolved. Increase heat to medium and bring mixture to a boil. Reduce heat and simmer, uncovered, about 10 minutes or until liquid is reduced by half.

Poach pears by gently stirring slices into wine sauce, coating fruit with liquid. Bring to a boil. Reduce heat and simmer, covered, for 3-5 minutes, stirring occasionally, until pears are tender. Do not overcook. Using a slotted spoon, place pears in a bowl; cover and chill for up to 24 hours.

Finish dessert in a 2-quart serving bowl. (Clear glass bowls are especially nice to show off trifles.) Alternate layers of the pumpkin bread cubes, pudding, and poached pear slices. Cover and chill for 4-6 hours. Before serving, top generously with whipped cream, a sprinkle of cinnamon, and lemon peel curls. Pass extra whipped cream to guests.

Serves 10-12

**Serve with Riesling.**

# Riesling Zabaglione

6    egg yolks
½    cup sugar
¼    cup Riesling wine
2    cups sliced fresh strawberries
     Whipped cream for garnish
4    strawberries, sliced in half, for garnish

In the top of double boiler over simmering water (bottom should not touch water), combine egg yolks, sugar, and wine. While cooking, use a portable electric mixer on low speed (or a hand-powered mixer) to blend ingredients for 5 minutes, or just until mixture mounds slightly. Remove top of double boiler from over water. Chill.

To serve, place ½ cup sliced strawberries in each of four stemmed dessert glasses. Spoon custard over top. Garnish with whipped cream and a half strawberry.

Serves 4

**Serve with Riesling.**

# Riesling Wine Custard

*If you're looking for a light dessert, try this custard made with wine instead of milk.*

2½   cups Late Harvest Riesling wine
¾    cup honey
1    strip orange zest
6    eggs
     Nutmeg for garnish

In a medium-sized saucepan over medium-high heat, combine the Riesling, honey, and orange zest; bring to a boil. Reduce heat and simmer, uncovered, for 10 minutes. Remove from heat and discard orange zest.

In a medium-sized heatproof bowl, lightly beat eggs. Whisk in hot wine mixture, pouring slowly at first in a thin stream, then more rapidly.

Pour the wine-egg mixture into 8 4-ounce ovenproof custard cups. Cover each with a small square of aluminum foil and press to seal around the rim.

Set custard cups on a steamer rack over simmering water. Cover and steam until the custard is just set but jiggles in the center when shaken, about 10 minutes. Let cool, then refrigerate. Serve cold, sprinkled with nutmeg.

Serves 8

**Serve with Late Harvest Riesling.**

80

# Riesling-Nectarine-Berry Ice

¾   cup Riesling wine
5   fresh nectarines
1   cup fresh or frozen red berries
1   cup whipped cream for garnish
     Fresh mint sprigs for garnish

Wash and peel nectarines. Purée in a food processor.

Wash berries and purée in a food processor.

In a large bowl, combine Riesling wine and puréed fruit; stir together. Freeze in a freezer container or in an ice cream maker according to manufacturer's directions.

Thirty minutes before serving, process fruit ice in food processor and refreeze. To serve, spoon into individual bowls. Top with a dollops of whipped cream and garnish with mint sprigs.

Serves 6-8

**Serve with Riesling.** Place a slice of nectarine or a few berries and a mint sprig in the wine glass for added flair.

# Riesling Cream with Strawberries

2    pints fresh ripe strawberries, halved
½    cup sugar
4¾    cups heavy cream (whipping cream)
2    cups sugar
2    packages unflavored gelatin
2    pints sour cream
¼    cup Late Harvest Riesling
     Whipped cream or creme fraiche (pg. 76) for garnish
     Finely chopped macadamia nuts for garnish

In a medium-sized bowl, combine the strawberry halves with sugar. Cover and refrigerate until ready to serve dessert.

In a medium-sized saucepan over medium-low heat, combine cream, sugar, and gelatin. Cook, stirring continuously, until gelatin is dissolved and liquid thickens slightly, about 5 minutes.

Remove from heat and gently fold in sour cream and Riesling wine. Pour into 6 dessert dishes and chill until firm, about 2 hours.

To serve, top each dessert with strawberries, a dollop of whipped cream, and a sprinkling of nuts.

Serves 6

**Serve with Late Harvest Riesling.**

# Riesling Rice Pudding

½   cup golden raisins
½   cup Late Harvest Riesling wine
3   cups cooked rice
2   medium apples, sliced
    Grated rind and juice of ½ orange
    Grated rind and juice of ½ lemon
2   egg yolks, beaten
½   cup sugar
1   teaspoon ground cinnamon
2   egg whites, beaten to soft peaks
    Whipped cream for garnish

**NOTE:** Soak raisins in Riesling wine for at least 1 hour to soften.

Preheat oven to 350° F.

In a large bowl, combine raisins, wine, cooked rice, apples, orange and lemon juices, egg yolks, sugar and cinnamon. Mix well.

Fold beaten egg whites into fruit-and-rice mixture. Pour into a greased, 8-inch round ovenproof bowl. Bake for 1 hour.

Serve warm with whipped cream, if desired.

Serves 6

**Serve with Late Harvest Riesling.**

# Late Harvest Apple Cake

½   cup Late Harvest Riesling
1   cup golden raisins
2¾   cups all-purpose flour
1½   teaspoons baking soda
1½   teaspoons cinnamon
½   teaspoon baking powder
½   teaspoon salt
½   teaspoon nutmeg
¼   teaspoon allspice
¾   cup sweet butter, at room temperature
1¾   cups sugar
3   large eggs, beaten
1¾   unsweetened applesauce

Preheat oven to 350° F. Coat the interior of a bundt pan with butter and sprinkle with flour.

In a small saucepan over medium high heat, bring Riesling wine to a gentle boil; add raisins and simmer, uncovered, for 10 minutes. Set aside.

In a medium bowl, mix all dry ingredients.

In a large bowl, beat butter and sugar together. In alternating fashion, add eggs and flour mixture to butter mixture. Fold in raisins and applesauce. Pour into buttered and floured bundt pan. Bake for 1 hour or until done.

Serves 8-12

**Serve with Late Harvest Riesling.**

# Riesling Lychee Sorbet

½    **cup water**
½    **cup sugar**
1    **pound fresh lychees (peeled, seeded, and puréed)**
     **or buy an 8-ounce can of lychees, puréed**
1    **teaspoon dried ginger**
¼    **cup Late Harvest Riesling**
½    **cup finely chopped macadamia nuts for garnish**
8    **mint leaves for garnish**

In a small saucepan over medium heat, combine water and sugar; simmer until sugar is dissolved. Let cool.

When syrup is cool, combine with the lychee purée, ginger, and Riesling wine.

Process in an ice cream maker according to manufacturer's instructions. Or, freeze in a freezer container, process in a blender, and refreeze.

To serve, spoon into individual bowls, sprinkle with chopped macadamia nuts, and add a touch of color with mint leaves.

Serves 4

**Serve with Late Harvest Riesling.**

# Poached Pear Ice Cream Sauce

| | |
|---|---|
| 1 | cup Late Harvest Riesling |
| 1 | tablespoon honey |
| ½ | teaspoon mace |
| ½ | teaspoon grated fresh lemon peel |
| ½ | teaspoon vanilla flavoring |
| 1 | teaspoon lemon juice |
| 4 | ripe but firm pears such as Comice, Bartlett or Bosc |
| | Chopped pecans for garnish |

In a medium saucepan over medium-high heat, bring wine, honey, mace, lemon peel, vanilla, and lemon juice to a boil. Simmer, uncovered, for 3 to 4 minutes. Set aside.

Peel pears, remove stem and core, and slice. Add pears to the wine mixture, cover, and simmer for 5 to 10 minutes, until pears are crisp-tender.

Serve the poached pears and syrup, warm or cold, over vanilla ice cream. Garnish with chopped pecans.

Serves 4

**Serve with Late Harvest Riesling.**

# Lazy Day Cobbler

¼   **pound (1 cube) butter**
1½  **cups sugar, divided**
1    **cup self-rising flour**
½   **cup milk**
½   **cup Riesling wine**
2    **cups peaches or apples, peeled and sliced**
½   **cup heavy cream, whipped**
      **Chopped walnuts for garnish**

Preheat oven to 400° F.

In a medium-sized bowl, combine ½ cup of the sugar with the fruit.

In an 8 x 8 x 2-inch baking pan over low heat, melt butter. Swirl pan to coat bottom and sides with butter.

In another medium-sized bowl, stir together the remaining 1-cup sugar, flour, milk, and Riesling wine. Pour flour mixture into melted butter, pressing to the sides of the pan to create a hollow center.

Pour the sweetened fruit and its juice into the center of the pan. Do not stir. Bake for 30 minutes or until browned.

Serve with whipped cream sprinkled with walnuts.

Serves 4

**Serve with Late Harvest Riesling.**

# Glossary and Pronunciation Guide

**Al dente (al DEN-tee; al-DEN-tay):** A term for pasta that is cooked until tender but not soft, having a firmness that is somewhat resistant to the teeth. Literally, "to the tooth" in Italian.

**Angel hair:** Pasta cut into thin, extremely long strands.

**Antipasto, Antipasti (pl.) (ahn-tee-PAHS-toh, ahn-tee-PAHS-tee):** A single hot of cold appetizer (antipasto) or an assortment (antipasti) served before a meal. Italian for "before the pasta."

**Au Gratin (oh GRAHT-n):** Food cooked with a top crust of bread crumbs and butter, sauce or grated cheese, and then browned in an oven.

**Basil (BAYZ-l):** A sweet, aromatic herb in the mint family that is cultivated for its leaves. When purchased fresh and not used immediately, basil will maintain its quality longer if it is placed in a container of water, stem ends down like a bouquet, and kept in the refrigerator. Basil is a main ingredient in pesto and is a popular seasoning in many modern recipes.

**To baste (BAY-st):** The process of spooning melted butter, hot fat, a sauce, or other liquid over meat as it roasts to keep it moist and juicy.

**Bay leaf:** The dried, aromatic leaf of the laurel or bay tree. It is normally used in a dried state as a flavoring for soups, stews, meats and other dishes, removed from the food prior to serving.

**To beat:** To stir rapidly with a circular motion, using a spoon, whisk, rotary beater or electric mixer, to give lightness to a mixture. Approximately 100 strokes by hand equals 1 minute by electric mixer.

**Beurre Blanc (burr BLAHN; burr BLAHNK:** A classic French wine sauce in which butter is whisked into the sauce until it is thick and smooth. Literally, "white butter" in French.

**Bisque (BISK):** A rich, creamy soup made from fish, shellfish, meat, or puréed vegetables.

**To blanch:** To plunge food (usually fruits and vegetables) into boiling water briefly, then into cold water to stop the cooking process. Blanching is generally used to partially cook foods before adding them to certain dishes, or to loosen the skin (as with tomatoes or peaches) for easy removal.

**To blend:** To stir a mixture until the ingredients are completely combined and smooth.

**Blue cheese:** A type of cheese that has been treated with molds that form blue or green veins throughout and give the cheese a strong flavor and aroma, both of which intensify with aging.

**To boil:** To immerse food in water, stock or other liquid when it has reached 212° F and is bubbling vigorously.

**Bouillon (BOOL-yon; BOO-yon):** A clear, thin broth made by simmering beef, chicken or vegetables with seasonings.
**Bouillon cube:** A small cube of evaporated seasoned meat, poultry or vegetable stock used to make broth or add flavor to soups, stews and other dishes. Bouillon cubes are packed in small containers and sold in grocery stores.

**Bouquet garni (boh-kay gar-nee):** Herbs (traditionally 2 or 3 stalks of parsley, a sprig of thyme, and a bay leaf) tied together with string, wrapped in cheesecloth, or enclosed in a small cloth sack, then immersed in soups and stews to add flavor. The bouquet is removed from the cooked food before serving.

**To braise (brayz):** To brown meat, vegetables, or other foods in hot fat, then cook them in a small amount of liquid in a tightly covered container at low heat for an extended period of time. Braising can be done on the stove top or in the oven.

**Caper (KAY-per):** A pickled flower bud of the caper bush. Packed in salt or vinegar and sold in grocery stores, the pungent condiment is used in sauces, relishes, and many other dishes.

**Cardamom (KAHR-deh-mehm)(-mehn):** The seeds of an Indian herb fruit, used as a spice or condiment.

**Casserole (KAS-eh-rohl):** A dish, usually of earthenware or glass, in which food is baked and served. Both the container and the food prepared in it are referred to as a casserole.

**Cayenne (KAI-yehn):** A hot powder made from a variety of tropical chiles, also known as red pepper.

**Cheddar cheese:** Any of several types of firm, smooth cheese made from cow's milk. Cheddar ranges in flavor from mild to extra sharp and is naturally white but is often colored with a natural orange dye. This popular cheese originated in the village of Cheddar in the Somerset region of England.

**Chervil (CHUR-vl):** A delicate fernlike herb often used to flavor sauces and vinegars (often in combination with tarragon) and as a garnish. A member of the parsley family, chervil leaves are sweeter and more aromatic than standard parsley.

**Chives (ch-eye-vs):** The leaves of a bulbous herb of the lily family, used as seasoning.

**Chowder:** A thick soup containing fish or shellfish and vegetables in a milk or tomato base. Or, a soup similar to this seafood dish.

**Chutney (CHUHT-nee):** A spicy condiment that ranges from mild to hot, made from fruit, vinegar, sugar, and spices. The name derives from the East Indian word *chatni*.

**Cilantro (see-LAHN-troh):** The Spanish name for coriander, from old Spanish alteration of the Latin *coriandrum*. It is widely used in Asian, Caribbean and Latin American cooking.

**Concassée (Kohn-kah-SAY):** A coarsely chopped, seasoned mixture, usually made from tomatoes that have been peeled and seeded.

**Coriander (KOHR-ee-an-der):** An aromatic herb in the parsley family. The fresh, pungent leaves of this plant (also called Chinese parsley and cilantro) are used in salads and other, especially highly seasoned. The seedlike fruit, used whole or ground, is used as a seasoning, as in curry powder.

**Cornstarch:** A very fine flour made from corn, largely used as a thickening agent.

**Creme Fraische (krehm FRESH):** A mixture of sour cream, powdered sugar, whipping cream, or other ingredients that has been allowed to ferment slightly, often used as a dessert topping or an ingredient in sauces. Literally, "fresh cream" in French.

**Crisp-tender:** Vegetables that are cooked until they are tender but not soft, having a fresh crispness that is somewhat resistent to the teeth.

**Croquette (kroh-KEHT):** A mixture of meat or vegatables, sauce and seasonings, which is formed into small rounds, dipped in beaten egg and bread crumbs, and deep fried.

**Crouton (KROO-tawn):** A slice or small cube of bread that has been baked or sautéed until brown, used as a garnish for soups, salads, and other dishes.

**Cumin (KOO-mihn):** A dried fruit of a plant in the parsley family whose aromatic, nutty-flavored seeds, which are available in seed and ground forms, are popular in Asian, Mediterranean and Middle Eastern cooking.

**Curry powder:** A pungent seasoning blended from chili, cinnamon, cumin, coriander, ginger, mustard, pepper, turmeric, and other spices. Curry powders are available from mild to hot depending on the amount of hotter spices used in the blend.

**Deglaze (dee-GLAYZ):** To dissolve the remaining bits of sautéed meat or roasted food and congealed juices from the bottom of a pan by adding a liquid and heating. First, the food is removed and excess fat discarded, then the remaining sediments are heated with stock, wine, or other liquid to make a gravy or sauce.

**Dijon (dee-ZHON):** A French city noted for its foodstuffs, including mustard.

**Dollop (DOLL-ehp):** A small quantity or splash.

**Dredge (DREJ):** To coat food by sprinkling it with flour, sugar, bread crumbs, or other powdery mixture or substance.

**Feta (FEHT-ah):** A semisoft white cheese usually made from goat's or ewe's milk and often preserved in brine, which gives it a slightly astringent and salty flavor. From the modern Greek *pheta*, "slice of cheese," and the Italian *fetta*, "slice."

**Fennel (FEN-l):** A Eurasian plant and its edible seeds or stalks, which have an anise flavor and are used to season foods.

**Fettucine (FET-eh-CHEE-nee):** Pasta cut into narrow flat strips, or a dish made with this pasta.

**Fillet (fih-LAY):** A strip or compact piece of boneless meat or fish.

**Fines herbes (feen ZEHRB, feen ehrb) :** A classic blend of finely chopped herbs, specifically chervil, chives, parsley, tarragon, and thyme, mixed together and used as a seasoning. Literally, "fine herbs" in French.

**Fricassee (FRIHK-uh-see):** A thick stew, usually made of chicken that has been sauteed in butter and cooked with vegetables and wine.

**To garnish:** To decorate prepared foods or beverages with small, colorful or savory items such as parsley, chopped scallions, flowers, mint leaves, or nuts.

**Genovese (jehn-oh-EEZ; jehn-oh-VEEZ):** Dishes prepared in the style of Genoa, an Italian seaport city.

**Green onion/scallion:** An immature onion harvested before the bulb has developed. Both the green stem and the immature white bulb are delicious and can be used in recipes.

**Gruyère (groo-YEHR):** A nutty, pale yellow, firm cheese made from cow's milk, named for its area of origin in Switzerland.

**Italian (ih-tal-yen):** From or characteristic of Italy. The "I" in "Italian" is pronounced like the "I" in "Italy" (IH-tal-ee).

**Jack cheese (also known as California Jack, Monterey Jack, and Sonoma Jack):** A versatile cheese made from cow's milk. **Unaged Jack** is ivory colored, semisoft in texture, and mildly flavored. It is widely available throughout the United States, plain or flavored with jalapeño pepper, garlic, dill or other seasonings. **Aged or Dry Jack** is yellow colored, firm textured, and sharper flavored and is generally found on ly on the West Coast or in specialty cheese shops.

**Jalapeño (ha-la-PEN-yo):** A spicy red or green pepper.

**Jarlsberg (YAHRLZ-berg):** A mild Norwegian cheese with a buttery, slightly sweet flavor. It is made in the style of Swiss cheese with large irregular holes and is excellent for cooking and snacking.

**Kosher salt:** A refined, coarse-grained salt that has no additives.

**Lasagna, lasagne (luh-ZAHN-yuh):** A wide, flat noodle, sometimes with ruffled edges. Also, a baked dish made by layering lasagna noodles with cheeses, fillings, and sauce.

**Leek:** A plant related to the onion.

**Linguine/linguini (lin-GWEE-nee):** Pasta cut into long, flat, thin strands.

**Lychee / litchi (LEE-chee):** An Asian fruit with creamy white flesh that is juicy, smooth, and sweet. Fresh lychees are availalbe in many areas from June to about mid-July but for most recipes, canned lychees, which are available year-round, will suffice.

**Lyonnais (lee-oh-NAY; li-uh-NAYZ; lee-oh-NEHZ):** Dishes prepared in the style of the city of Lyon, France.

**Macaroni (mac-ah-ROH-nee):** Any of several types of hollow pasta, especially short curved tubes.

**Mace (may-s):** An aromatic spice derived from the dried, lacy, outer coating of the nutmeg kernel. Mace and nutmeg can be used interchangeably.

**Maraschino (mar-ah-SKEE-no) cherries:** Sweet pitted cherries that are tinted with red food coloring and preserved in a sugar syrup. The name is derived from the Italian marasca cherry and the maraschino cordial made from the cherry's fermented juice and crushed pits.

**Marjoram (MAR-jer-em):** A spicy aromatic herb whose leaves are used for seasoning, especially popular in bread stuffing and with lamb.

**Marinade (MARE-eh-nayd):** A liquid combination, usually vinegar or wine, oil, and various herbs and spices, in which meat or vegetables are soaked before cooking.

**Meringue (meh-RANG):** A light, airy topping made of egg whites and sugar that is beaten until stiff, spread on pastry or pies, and baked until brown.

**Mousse (MOOS):** A rich, light, airy dish that takes its name from the French word for "froth" or "foam." A mousse can be a chilled, sweet dessert or a hot, savory dish. Fluffiness results from adding whipped cream or beaten egg whites.

**Mozzarella (mot-seh-REL-eh):** A mild, white Italian cheese with a rubbery texture, often eaten melted on pizza and in Italian dishes. From the Italian *mozzare*, "to cut off."

**Nutmeg:** A sweet, nutty spice derived from the seed of the East Indies nutmeg tree. Grated or ground, nutmeg is popularly used in cakes, cookies, custards and white sauces.

**Pancetta (pahn-CHET-ah):** Italian bacon that has been cured in salt and spices and then air-dried.

**To pare:** To remove a very thin layer from the outer covering or skin of fruits or vegetables with a knife or vegetable peeler.

**Parmesan (PAR-meh-zahn):** A hard, sharp, dry Italian cheese made from skim milk. Its dry texture is ideal for grating or as a garnish. It originated in Parma, Italy.

**Pilaf (pih-LAHF; PEE-lahf):** A steamed rice dish often made with meat, seafood or vegetables in a seasoned broth.

**Pimiento (pih-mee-EHN-toh; pih-MEN-toh):** A large, red, aromatic sweet pepper. Fresh pimientos are available in specialty stores and farmers markets from late summer to early fall. Canned and bottled pimientos, which are popularly used in cooking, salads, and stuffing green olives, are available year-round. Literally, "pepper" in Spanish.

**Piquant (PEE-kehnt; pee-KAHNT):** Tasting pleasantly spicy, pungent or tart. From the Old French *piquer*, "to prick."

**To poach:** To cook gently in simmering liquid so that the cooked food retains its shape.

**Polenta:** A thick mush made of cornmeal boiled in water or stock.

**Porcini (pohr-CHEE-nee) mushroom:** A wild mushroom that is pale brown in color and weighs from 1 to 16 ounces with caps ranging from 1 to 10 inches in diameter. Sometimes available in specialty markets, it is easier to find in dried form, which must be softened in hot water for about 20 minutes before using.

**Proscuitto (pro-SHOO-toh):** An aged, dry, spicy Italian ham that is usually sliced thin and served without cooking.

**Purée (pyoo-RAY):** Fruit, vegetables, meat or other food (usually precooked) that is rubbed through a strainer, sieved, or blended in a food processor to a thick cream.

**Quenelles (kuh-NEHL):** A light dumpling made of seasoned minced or ground meat, fish, or vegetables and egg, formed into small ovals and poached in stock.

**Radiatore (rah-dyah-TOH-ray):** Short, rippled-edged pasta pieces that resembles small radiators. Literally, "little radiators" in Italian.

**Ragout (ra-GOO):** A stew in which the meat is usually browned before stewing, made from pieces of meat or fish that are cooked slowly without thickening.

**To reduce:** To diminish the quantity and improve the quality of a sauce or other cooking liquid by gently boiling until it becomes thicker and the flavor more concentrated.

**Ricotta (rih-KAHT-ah):** A soft, bland, fresh cheese that resembles cottage cheese, popularly used in lasagna, canneloni, and other Italian dishes. From the Latin *rococta* and *recoquere*, "to cook again."

**Riesling (REEZ-ling, REES-ling):** A delicate but complex white wine made from Riesling grapes or a blend of Riesling and other grape varieties.

**Romano (roh-MAH-noh) cheese:** A very firm, pale yellow cheese generally used in a grated form. Named for the city of Rome in which they originated, there are several different styles of Romano cheese, made with sheep's, goat's, or cow's milk and varying from mild to very sharp.

**Roux (ROO):** A fat-and-flour mixture that is cooked together and used to thicken sauces. There are three types of roux – white, blond and brown. White roux is not cooked after the flour is added, blond roux is cooked until straw-colored, and brown roux is cooked until it is a dark brown color.

**Saffron (SAF-ruhn):** A pungent, aromatic, yellow spice made from stigmas of a small purple crocus (*Crocus sativus*), popularly used to flavor risotto, bouillabaisse, and paella. Saffron is available in powdered form and threads and is the world's most expensive spice.

**Sage (SAYJ):** Any of several native Mediterranean plants with grayish-green, aromatic leaves that are used as seasonings, commonly in dishes containing pork, cheese and beans, and in poultry and game stuffings.

**To sauté (saw-TAY):** To fry foods lightly in fat in a shallow open pan. Also, sauté refers to any dish prepared in this manner.

**Scallion/green onion:** An immature onion harvested before the bulb has developed. Both the green stem and the immature white bulb are delicious and can be used in recipes.

**Scallopini (skal-eh-PEE-nee):** Small, thinly sliced pieces of met, especially veal, dredged in flour, sautéed and served in sauce.

**Scallops:** Small, white shellfish that grow in fan-shaped shells with a radiating fluted pattern. 1) **Bay scallops** have a sweet, nutlike flavor and are relatively scarce; 2) **sea scallops** have a robust taste and are more widely available.

**Sea salt:** Salt produced by the evaporation of sea water and that contains sodium chloride and trace elements such as sulfur, magnesium, zinc, potassium, calcium, and iron, generally used in a coarse state.

**Seasoning:** Salt, pepper, herbs and other flavorings used in cooking. To "adjust" or "correct" seasoning is to taste the food near the end of the cooking period to see seasonings are needed, then to add more to suit your taste.

**Shallot (SHALL-et):** A type of onion whose mild-flavored bulb is used in soups, sauces, stews, and other dishes. Shallots grow like garlic in a cluster on a common vine.

**Simmer:** To cook liquid gently at about 195° F or remain just at or below the liquid's boiling point.

**Sorbet (sor-BAY):** A lightly sweetened or savory frozen dish made without milk, usually served either as a dessert or a palate refresher between courses.

**To steam:** To cook food by placing it on a rack in a closed container and exposing the food to moist steam heat (pressurized water vapor), being careful to keep the food away from boiling water below it.

**Stock:** A broth made by simmering meat, bones, poultry, vegetables or fish for several hours, used as a base in preparing soup, stew, gravy, or sauces.

**Stuffing, dressing:** A mixture of savory ingredients, usually highly seasoned, used to fill cavities in fish, poultry, or meat, or cooked separately. Although the terms are often used interchangeably, more precisely, *stuffing* is cooked inside the meat, fish, or poultry; *dressing* is cooked in a dish or pan.

**Sun-dried tomatoes:** Tomatoes dried in the sun (or by artificial methods), which intensifies flavor, sweetness, and color. They are chewy (like dried fruit), and are usually packed in oil or dry-packed in cellophane. Sun-dried tomatoes add delicious flavor dimensions to a wide variety of dishes.

**Swiss cheese:** A firm white or pale yellow cheese with a nutlike flavor and many holes, originally produced in Switzerland.

**To tenderize:** To break down tough meat fibers, usually by marinating or beating it with a mallet.

**Thyme (TYME):** Any of several aromatic herbs whose leaves are used in *bouquet garni* and as a seasoning in soups, vegetables, stews, poultry, and other dishes.

**Tomato paste:** A rich, sweet concentrate made from tomatoes that have been cooked for several hours, strained, and reduced. It is available in cans and tubes. **Tomato sauce**, available in cans, is a less sweet, thin tomato purée.

**Turmeric (TER-mer-ihk; TOO-mer-ihk):** An Indian plant whose powdered rhizomes are used as a condiment.

**Water chestnut:** The white, mild, crunchy tuber of an Asian plant, especially popular in stir-fried dishes, availalbe fresh or canned.

**Watercress:** A member of the mustard family that has crisp, dark green leaves and a pungent flavor, generally sold in small bouquets.

**To whisk:** To beat quickly with a light circular motion, using a hand-held metal whisk or rotary beater, or an electric mixer, to incorporate air (fluffiness) into eggs, cream, or food mixtures.

**White pepper:** A less pungent pepper ground from peppercorns from which the outer black layer has been removed, popular for use in light-colored sauces and foods.

**White sauce:** A sauce made with butter, flour, and milk, cream, or stock, used as a base for other sauces.

**Wine**

>**appellation (ap-peh-LAY-shuhn):** A protected name under which a wine may be sold, indicating that grapes used are of a specific kind from a specific district.

>**aroma:** The smell or fragrance of the wine.

>**body:** The perception of texture or consistency of a wine in the mouth.

>**bouquet (boh-KAY):** A unique and complex fragrance that emerges when a wine is fermented and aged.

>**complexity:** A complex wine has myriad layers and nuances of bouquet and flavor.

>**dry:** Dry wine has very little or no sweetness. In a *fully dry* wine, all sugar has been converted to alcohol during fermentation. A *medium-dry* wine contains a small amount of sugar, and an *off-dry* wine has the barest hint of sweetness. A wine may be both dry and fruity.

>**estate bottled:** The winery either owns or controls the vineyard and is responsible for the growing of the grapes used in the wine.

>**finish; aftertaste:** The flavor characteristics of a wine that remain in the mouth and nasal passages after a wine has been swallowed.

**nose:** A wine's scent or fragrance. "A good nose" means the wine has a fine bouquet and aroma.

**sweet:** Sweet wine may result naturally from the amount of sugar in the grapes at harvest, or sweetness may be supplemented by the wine maker.

**texture:** Wine that is perceived as intense and full-bodied, producing a dense impression on the palate that makes the wine seem almost thick.

**varietal (vehr-EYE-ih-tl):** A wine named for the grape from which it is made. Although one or more grape varieties may be used in making a varietal, by United States law, the wine must be blended from at least 75 percent of the named varietal.

**vintage (VIHN-tihj):** The year grapes were grown and harvested. In the United States, the wine label may list the vintage year if 95 percent of the wine comes from grapes harvested that year.

**viticultural (VIHT-ih-kuhl-cher-uhl) area:** A region where grapes are grown.

**Worcestershire (WOOS-ter-sheer; WOOS-ter-sher):** A rich-bodied, piquant sauce of soy, vinegar, and spices, originating in the borough of Worcester (WOO-ster), England.

**Yogurt (YOH-gehrt):** A custardlike food with a tart flavor made from milk curdled by bacteria, often sweetened or flavored. From the Turkish *yogur*, "to knead."

**Zabaglione (zah-bahl-YOH-nay):** An light Italian dessert made from egg yolks, wine, and sugar, cooked over simmering water until a light, foamy custard is formed. There is also a frozen version.

**Zucchini (zoo-KEE-nee):** A variety of elongated, dark green squash. From the Italian *zucca*, "gourd."

# INDEX

### ☆ Cooking With Wine
by Virginia and Robert Hoffman

Eighty-six American winery chefs share 172 of their best recipes for cooking with wine and pairing food with wine in this excellent cookbook. Whether you are a novice or an expert in the kitchen, you'll enjoy these great recipes. But that's not all. You'll also learn how cooking with wine can be good for your health! Included is a glossary of American wines and suggested pairings of wine and food. This bestselling cookbook is considered a classic.

ISBN 0-9629927-3-9, softcover, 206 pages    **$15.95**

### ☆ The Great Little Food With Wine Cookbook, 2nd Edition
by Virginia and Robert Hoffman

There's a lot of information in this cookbook! You'll enjoy excellent recipes by some of America's finest winery chefs, tips on how and where to buy wine, guidelines for selecting wine in restaurants, helpful hints on deciphering wine labels so you know what you're buying, and how to select wines to go with your meals ... and the wines are all American.

ISBN 1-877810-70-3, softcover, 128 pages    **$9.95**

## ☆ *The California Wine Country Cookbook II*
### by Virginia and Robert Hoffman

Here are 172 exciting recipes from the most creative chefs of the California wine country. Recipes for appetizers, soups, salads, pastas, meats, seafood, poultry, vegetables and desserts — each an exciting addition to your culinary repertoire. Some recipes are quite simple, easy and fast to prepare. Others require more time and effort. All are innovative and will bring the cuisine of the California Wine Country into your home.

ISBN 0-9629927-6-3, softcover, 208 pages     **$12.95**

## ☆ *The California Wine Country Herbs & Spices Cookbook, New Revised Edition*
### by Virginia and Robert Hoffman

Herbs and spices are the theme of this collection of recipes by 96 of the foremost chefs in the California wine country. You'll enjoy 212 of the best recipes that made them world famous for their cuisine. You'll discover exciting new ways to use 37 herbs and spices, how to make your own spice mixes, and how to make herbed and spiced oils and vinegars.

ISBN 0-9629927-7-1, softcover, 240 pages     **$14.95**

## ☆ *Great Salsas!*
### by Virginia and Robert Hoffman

This collection of 96 salsa recipes takes you from mild and mellow to very hot. Discover delicious recipes from Latin America, the Caribbean, Africa, the Far East, and the American Southwest. Each is simple and easy to make ... and guaranteed to tantalize your taste buds. Come with us on a culinary adventure using exotic but easy-to-find ingredients, and enjoy new and exciting flavors, aromas to make your mouth water, and excitement in every taste!

ISBN 1-893718-05-0, softcover, 96 pages     **$7.95**

## ☆ *The Wine-Lover's Holidays Cookbook*
by Virginia and Robert Hoffman

You'll enjoy happier holidays with this timesaving collection of menus, recipes and wine recommendations. There are 13 seasonal holiday menus, with recipes and suggested American wines to accompany them, for Thanksgiving, Christmas, Chanukah, Passover, Easter and the 4th of July. Each is easy to prepare and appropriate for the selected holiday. This charming book is a perfect gift or remembrance for any special occasion.

ISBN 1-893718-03-4, softcover, 144 pages    **$9.95**

## ☆ *Pairing Wine With Food*
by Virginia and Robert Hoffman

In this handy bestseller, more than 500 foods are paired with American wines. You'll learn where and how to buy wine, how to select wine in a restaurant, and even the right wines to pair with fast- and takeout foods. In addition, there's a helpful guide to American wines, and even a Winespeak Dictionary. With this book, you'll discover everything you've always wanted to know about pairing wine with food ... and more.

ISBN 1-893718-01-8, softcover, 96 pages    **$8.95**

## ☆ *Nancy's Candy Cookbook, 2nd Edition: How to Make Candy at Home the Easy Way*
by Nancy Shipman

Have fun and save money by making top-quality candy at home. In this step-by-step guidebook, candy specialist Nancy Shipman takes you through the candy-making process. There are more than 100 candy recipes plus information on ingredients, candy-making equipment, dipping and coating, and much more. You'll become an expert candy maker in no time. How sweet it is!

ISBN 1-877810-65-7, softcover, 192 pages    **$14.95**

## ☆ Cooking with Chardonnay:
## 75 Sensational Chardonnay Recipes
by Barbara and Norm Ray

Chardonnay is one of the most popular white table wines worldwide. Its unique flavors are ideal for drinking and cooking, many excellent vintages are readily available at reasonable prices, and it pairs well· with today's lighter cuisine. In this cookbook you'll enjoy 75 sensational, easy-to-prepare recipes, each of which is flavored with Chardonnay — soups, pastas and grains, meats, poultry, seafood, and desserts. In addition, you'll appreciate the introduction to Chardonnay, helpful guides on how to cook with wine, decipher wine labels, and serve wine, a glossary and pronunciation guide for wine cooking terms ... and more.

ISBN 1-877810-54-1, softcover, 128 pages    **$9.95**

## ☆ Cooking with Merlot:
## 75 Marvelous Merlot Recipes
by Barbara and Norm Ray

If you, your family, and friends enjoy moderately heavy cuisine with rich wine overtones, think Merlot! This exciting cookbook contains 75 marvelous, easy-to-prepare recipes, each of which is flavored with Merlot — soups, pastas and grains, meats, poultry, seafood, and desserts. In addition, there's an introduction to Merlot, helpful guides on how to cook with Merlot, decipher wine labels, and serve wine, a glossary and pronunciation guide for wine cooking terms ... and more.

ISBN 1-877810-53-3, softcover, 128 pages    **$9.95**

### ☆ Cooking with Riesling:
### 75 Remarkable Riesling Recipes
by Barbara and Norm Ray

Riesling wines, which range from very dry to very sweet, are praised for their delicate yet complex characteristics and their delightful versatility. Rieslings are delicious alone, in cooking, or as an accompaniment to a wide variety of foods, from mild appetizers to spicy exotic cuisine. In this excellent new cookbook, you'll discover for yourself Riesling's remarkable versatility as you choose from among 75 delicious recipes that feature Riesling. And, as in the other books in this series, *Cooking with Riesling* contains an introduction to Riesling wines, helpful guides on how to cook with wine, decipher wine labels, and serve wine, a glossary and pronunciation guide for wine cooking terms ... and more.

ISBN 1-877810-56-8, softcover, 128 pages    **$9.95**

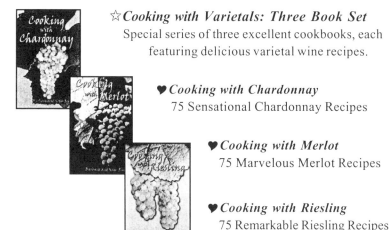

### ☆ Cooking with Varietals: Three Book Set
Special series of three excellent cookbooks, each featuring delicious varietal wine recipes.

### ♥ Cooking with Chardonnay
75 Sensational Chardonnay Recipes

### ♥ Cooking with Merlot
75 Marvelous Merlot Recipes

### ♥ Cooking with Riesling
75 Remarkable Riesling Recipes

ISBN 1-877810-63-0   Shrinkwrapped set of all 3 books   **$28.50**

# ORDER

To order Hoffman Press cookbooks through the mail, please complete this order form and forward with check, money order or credit card information to Rayve Productions, POB 726, Windsor CA 95492. If paying with a credit card, you can call us toll-free at 800.852.4890 or fax this completed form to Rayve Productions at 707.838.2220.

We invite you to visit our website and view our cookbooks at foodandwinebooks.com.

☐ Please send me the following book(s):

Title_____ Price_____ Qty____ Amount _____

Title_____ Price_____ Qty____ Amount _____

| | |
|---|---|
| **Quantity Discount: 4 items@10%;** **7 items@15%; 10 items@20%** | Subtotal $_____ <br> Discount $_____ |

|  |  |
|---|---|
| Subtotal | $_____ |

**Sales Tax**: Californians please add 7.5% sales tax
**Shipping & Handling**:
Book rate — $3 for first book + $1 each additional
Priority — $5 for first book + $1 each additional

| | |
|---|---|
| Sales Tax | $_____ |
| Shipping | $_____ |
| Total | $_____ |

Name _____ Phone _____

Address _____

City State Zip _____

☐ Check enclosed $ _____          Date _____

☐ Charge my Visa/MC/Discover/AMEX $_____

Credit card # _____          Exp. _____

Signature _____ *Thank you!* CWM03